GLIMPSES OF ATLANTIS

BIGFOOT & ALIENS

Glimpses of Atlantis, Bigfoot & Aliens:
You Are Not Going Crazy; You Are Awakening

This publication is designed to entertain the reader. All descriptions of events were real events. Names of characters have been changed for anonymity of the participants.

Book Cover by Dragon Clan Media via Adobe Firefly AI, Adobe Photoshop, and Adobe Illustrator.
Chapter Start Illustrations by Matthew Alexander.
Detailed Renditions within the book generated by Adobe Firefly AI software prompted by Matthew Alexander. Generated images were then modified in Adobe Photoshop 2024 by Matthew Alexander.
PRINT ISBN: 979-8-992-7308-0-7
EBOOK ISBN: 979-9927308-1-4

1st Edition 2025

WWW.DRAGONCLANMEDIA.COM

GLIMPSES OF ATLANTIS
BIGFOOT & ALIENS

YOU ARE NOT GOING CRAZY;
YOU ARE AWAKENING

MATTHEW ALEXANDER

To my wife and past lives partner in this and every universe.

To my children for teaching me how to focus on the now.

To my parents for giving me a safe and loving environment to learn and grow.

I HAVE COME TO REALIZE THAT THE ONLY DIFFERENCE BETWEEN A SKEPTIC OF THE PARANORMAL AND A BELIEVER IS THAT THE SKEPTIC HAS YET TO HAVE AN EXPERIENCE.

Acknowledgements

I really must thank my parents for not putting down my fascination with cryptids in my youth. Like so many of us, I knew the Paranormal section of our town's library like the back of my hand. Loch Ness monster, bigfoot, ghosts, and UFO's, I checked out most of those books during our summer breaks. Shows like *Unsolved Mysteries, Monster Quest, Ghost Hunters*, and the venerable Leonard Nimoy's *In Search Of* were shows that held my obsession.

Next, I want to send huge kudos to my dear friend and Vietnam Veteran, Doug. Not only did Doug and his wife, Susan, help take care of my wife during the years I had to travel the US for work for weeks at a time, but Doug is my buddy. We enjoyed many an overpriced beer and martial arts fight on television for years. But most importantly, Doug kept recommending meditation to me. It was Doug who planted the seed and helped begin my exploration into consciousness which seemed to reawaken so much supernatural that I had blocked for decades.

Also, I want to thank Dolores Cannon for her development of the Quantum Hypnosis Healing Technique (QHHT) and the decades she spent collecting sessions and releasing them in her many books. Along these lines, I must thank Abby, Margie, Sarah, Suzanne, and Kristy for helping me along this path. I want to thank all my soul friends that attended the Jupiter weekend.

CONTENTS

FORWARD

Using my journals as a vehicle, this book is largely an examination of consciousness through meditation, and aspects of what new physics refer to as quantum entanglement and wormholes. New understandings of different dimensions, esoteric connections, and encounters with everything from mythical beasts to cryptological mystery creatures, to extra-terrestrials or extra-dimensional beings or aliens to just lump them all together. Honestly, I think the term Non-Human Entity might be the best description, but the current vernacular still focuses on the term alien. Which I much prefer over the federal government trying to push us to use Non-Human Biologics in the same way they are pushing the term UAP over the tried-and-true UFO terminology. I believe these are moves by the government to control the narrative, so I won't be using their terms.

Regardless of all that, the reason I believe this is a worthy exploration is because of my and others experiences with the supernatural. Then we have the fascinating case of the billionaire space explorer Robert Bigelow. This man is the founder of Bigelow Aerospace and has had many federal contracts over the decades for space related jobs with NASA. He has also launched two space stations back in 2006 and 2007; thus, he has been in this game for a long time.

This is where it gets interesting, in 1995, Bigelow founded the National Institute for Discovery Science (NIDS). This institute was for funding the study of non-socially accepted sciences such as paranormal research and specifically a focus on ufology. This group researched cattle mutilations, UFO reports, and even inter-dimensional entities at the now infamous Skinwalker Ranch in Utah from 1996 to 2016. Along with researching at least one other site known as Bradshaw Ranch near Sedona, Arizona.

It was at Bradshaw Ranch where, reportedly, Bigelow had what might have been a life changing event happen to him. While on the ranch, sleeping in one of the rooms, a massively tall entity appeared in the corner of his room. It supposedly scared Bigelow so much that he immediately put the ranch up for sale and halted the onsite research.

In 2020, Bigelow completely shifts gears from UFOs to consciousness. He shut down Bigelow Aerospace that year and let's go his 88 employees, and he opens the Bigelow Institute for Consciousness Studies. He even posts an award of $1 million asking for essays arguing the existence of a life after death. The institute awarded three people money summing up to the million dollars.

If a billionaire dead set on proving the existence of UFOs for 20 years suddenly stops that venture to examine consciousness and the spirit realm, I think we should all stop and take notice. This is especially true when it costs us nothing to meditate and examine our consciousness.

I grew up attending a private Episcopal grammar school in California. We were not a religious family, and my parents told my brother and I that if we wanted to attend church, they would take us. We didn't. But, at school we had a bible lesson every morning before the school day. By the time I was thirteen, I had seen enough of organized religion. Some of the people in the faith around me were blatant hypocrites. Then I attended my friend's Catholic Church a few times. The rituals the priest runs the attendants through seemed like an obvious means of exerting control over people. Sorry if that interpretation offends you.

Thus, by the time I was a young teenager, I considered myself an atheist. God or Source did not exist. College only made me reject spirituality even more as I attained a Master's degree in genetics and evolution. But it was the field research that I did for my thesis that unwittingly put me in contact with the supernatural through the travels I conducted to collect research data.

Looking back on those years, I wish I had been as spiritual then as I have become in the last few years. I would have probably been able to gather more evidence of everything from Bigfoot to ETs.

Living most of my life as an atheist before my 'spiritual awakening', sure of the tenants of science and evolution, I thought all living beings be it plant or animal, were merely carbon entities that would break down upon death and return to the basic elements. No life after death.

Oh, how I was proven wrong over the last few years.

Being trained as a scientist, I have spent much of the last couple of years seeking confirmation of the things I've experienced by comparing notes between psychics I've worked with and then discussing these things with like-minded people. Much of my spare time has been spent researching everything from ghosts to cryptid creatures to ETs and I will interject correlations related to these throughout this book.

So, if you have an open mind and especially if you are beginning to question your own sanity as more of the spiritual opens to you, then please join me on this journey of spiritual awakening. Where the weird and fantastical rams into the mundane and sometimes painful life of the 21st century and the 3D world. Where I share my experiences with the metaphysical, spiritual, supernatural, and the weird; and some of the lessons that I have learned along the way. But ultimately, I hope this book will help those new to their own spiritual awakening. I hope to let you know that you are not crazy, and you should embrace the spiritual and explore your consciousness and see where it takes you.

If a former atheist and scientist like me can embrace the strangeness beyond what humans can see with their eyes, then others should be emboldened to walk down their own path to happy enlightenment.

CHAPTER 1

A WAKE-UP CALL

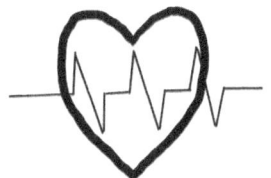

FEBRUARY 9, 2022

I found myself in a sterile doctor's office of a local clinic. I hated the doctor's office…and the dentist for that matter.

The door opened and a female entered. Dressed in the standard garb of the medical profession, white lab coat, stethoscope around her neck, laptop clutched to her chest. This was Physician's Assistant Heather. She's young, but I like her, and she actually has some bed side manner when so many actual doctors eschewed that part of their profession shortly after graduating from med school.

"Good morning, Mr. Alexander," Heather said.

"Hey, Doc, how are you?"

"I'm good, thank you. So, what seems to be the problem?"

"Well, my anxiety is under control with the medication you gave me, but I'm not sleeping well. I'm waking multiple times a night and I feel exhausted every morning."

"Are you waking to urinate?" She asked.

"Sometimes, but not always. I think some of it may be the dog moving on the bed or my wife coming to bed after I'm asleep. But there seems to be some other reason, and I don't have much of a guess as to what that could be," I said.

Looking at the screen on her laptop, Heather scrolled up and down for a bit. I fidgeted a little, uncomfortable on the crappy examine table they make you sit on.

"Well, there are a few things going on here based on your recent blood and urine results. You are 226 pounds right now, right?"

"Yeah, unfortunately," I replied with a grimace.

"I'm curious, how much did you weigh in your late twenties after you had been out of college for a while?"

"Well, I didn't actually finish my Master's degree until I was twenty-nine." That has always been a bit of an embarrassment on my part. Most people that stay in college until their late twenties end up with a PhD.

"Okay," Heather said, "How much did you weigh at thirty?"

"I was a pretty steady 186 during college and afterwards." I was proud of that, but I knew what was coming.

"Hmmm, well, you are forty-six now, but for being 6'2", your current weight of 226 is much too high." She said. "I would say you are about 30 pounds overweight. Given that, it isn't surprising that you have high blood pressure, especially with your family background, and with the extra weight, you might have sleep apnea too."

"Ugh," I moaned. "I really don't want to test for that. The insurance companies are vultures and I'm a side sleeper. So, I don't see how I could both start sleeping on my back and sleep with a freaking mask on my face."

"Well, sleep apnea could take years off your life if it is not treated,"

Heather said matter-of-factly, her normal bedside manner disappearing. This told me she was being serious.

"Well, with my wonky work schedule and my kid's hockey schedule, I don't have many opportunities to workout. What else can we do that doesn't involve increasing my blood pressure meds?"

"You coach your kids' hockey don't you," she asked, genuinely interested. Her bedside manner had returned.

"Yeah, my son, I coach his team full time, and my daughter is a goalie like I was. So, I work with her and the other goalies her age to help them work on the basics. It's fun, but it's five days a week plus their games on the weekends." I wasn't complaining. I genuinely love being on the ice helping the kids. Maybe it's the teacher in me, or my love for the sport, but I do cherish my time on the ice with my kids both in practice and in games. Although my daughter's games as goalie are getting a lot more stressful!

"Matt, if you don't have time to exercise, then that makes it that much more important for you to eat healthy."

"That is nearly impossible with the travel and long season these kids have these days in travel hockey leagues," I complained.

Heather looked up from her laptop. "Have you tried yoga or meditation to lower your anxiety and blood pressure?"

"Huh, meditation is interesting. My old Vietnam vet buddy tells me I should meditate. He said meditation helped his PTSD immensely." It was a funny way to make me think of my old friend, Doug. He lives on the other side of the country now, and I don't see him much anymore. Mostly just a random text here and there about fishing, expensive beers, or the latest Mixed Martial Arts fight coming up on Pay Per View. But for a guy that was thirty plus years older than me, we really hit it off and had a lot of things in common.

"You have to change something if you want to be around to see your kids go to college and get married someday," Heather said, dropping her bedside manner again.

"Okay," I said, suddenly feeling really sobered. "I guess cutting back on the alcohol will help too, huh?"

"Oh yeah," she said, her eyes wide. "I don't like your liver numbers for your age. And you have admitted to me that you have drank too much during the last three years of the pandemic. Right?"

"Yep, I borderline have a problem." It's funny, I am too honest for my own good. It is why I have had few friends my entire life. I speak what's on my mind. Because of it my wife and partner of twenty-five years and a couple friends are the only ones to stick with me over time.

Heather looked at me out of the corner of her eyes. "So, what are you telling me?"

"I'm telling you that I'm going to quit drinking as much, and I'm going to look into this meditation thing." I wasn't lying, but I also wanted to escape the wrath of my medical professional.

CHAPTER 2

MEDITATION

Meditation. It is just sitting and thinking about rivers or the beach, right?

Not sure where to start, I decided the best bet would be to scroll through free guided meditations on my phone. But nothing really grabbed me. Then I remembered a fascinating character in the UFO world had an app with some meditations. Yes, UFOs are a guilty pleasure of mine for as long as I can remember. Throw in some Bigfoot and ghost stories and I'm entertained.

It didn't take long to find his app and download it. Scrolling through the half dozen meditations he offered; I found one about the Universe. Things don't get more profound than that, and at thirty minutes maybe it will give me enough time to experience whatever it is that people promoting meditation swear by. So, I tracked down my headphones and decided on a chair that my lower back and sciatica pain could likely handle for that long and gave it a try. Three lower back surgeries for herniated discs will limit a person's ability to sit comfortably in just any old chair. Because there is no way I could sit on the ground like you see people doing other meditate.

"*NOW*," boomed the narrator's voice, "close your eyes and let's be in a relaxed state..."

Damn, if that wasn't an impressive start to my roller coaster ride of meditation and eventual spiritual awakening!

The narrator guided me into a deep state of meditation. Something I would later learn is called the Theta brainwave state. There are five brain states recognized by science today. Ranging from higher frequency range called Gamma, which corresponds to concentration. Down to the slowest frequency which is sleep, or Delta. Theta is one step above sleep and described as being deeply relaxed or inwardly focused. This is the hole-in-one of meditation and somehow, I hit it on my first try.

That is when the proverbial shit hit the fan.

With my eyes closed, I saw what practitioners and psychics, or woo folks in general, describe as images in my mind's eye. I saw my body blast up from my house, into the upper atmosphere, bursting into the darkness of space and blasting past our moon. But it didn't end there, somehow, I shot into a Star Wars or Star Trek type speed of light wackiness. I felt like I was going deep into the universe until I slammed to a halt. I felt that I was floating.

Everything around me was black with red enveloping it. Everything related to these red lines like a galactic spiderweb. It was so incredible I would have cried if I wasn't so awestruck.

After whom knows how long, I became cognizant of my narrator's prompts again and felt pulled back to Earth and my heavy body. In a flash I was back above Earth. Only this time the red cosmic spiderweb was still present. The red lines spread out from my red energy body to the moon, the sun, the Earth, to everything. As my body drifted down to Earth as a feather gently floats from a bird, I could see EVERYTHING was connected. Red threads connected everything to everything. Trees connected to animals, to grass, to humans, to rocks, to insects, and on and on.

I got the sense that I was being shown this profound scene to impress upon me that everything, no matter how seemingly insignificant, is connected. I would later come to understand that everything has consciousness, even rocks, and everything is ONE.

There are lots of ideas about what consciousness is and how it works. However, in my opinion there are really two main camps of thought about consciousness. I am going to be very simplistic as this is a complicated topic. I don't want to espouse on it too much as I want to explore it in real time instead of philosophizing about it.

One camp being the nuts-and-bolts science/medical camp. These scientists believe that consciousness is closely related to the belief that the brain is an electronic machine of sorts. Neurons in different parts of the brain are excited and via electrical and magnetic pulses and how we interpret them is the extent of consciousness. All very mundane, nothing Woo.

The other camp being the spiritual camp. Spiritual can describe anything esoteric or metaphysical, ranging from belief in a single god, many gods, some kind of sentient 'creator' of the universe, to the idea of everything coming from a single source of energy. So, whether a person calls this 'higher power' God by any specific religion's naming system or Source, it is ultimately the same thing just with nuanced differences.

CHAPTER 3

IS THIS WHY PEOPLE MEDITATE?

FEBRUARY 13, 2022

After that first meditation, I found myself relaxed but strangely exhausted. To the point I dragged myself out of my chair and slumped into my bed. I passed out almost immediately.

Sometime later, my wife came in and woke me.

"What are you sleeping for?" My wife asked. "It's not even noon yet."

"Ugh, yeah." I almost struggled to roll over and sit up. "I just did a meditation on my phone and afterwards I felt like I couldn't function. It was nap or nothing."

Jennifer looked at Matt from the corner of her eyes as she folded laundry.

I didn't feel comfortable talking to her about what I had seen in my head. But for some reason I suddenly remembered my one ghost encounter. "Remember the ghost in Costa Rica?"

"The ghost girl that crawled in bed with you. Ha, yeah, I remember. I don't think I've seen you that scared before or since."

Thinking on it, that was the first time I had experienced 'seeing' something in my mind's eye. We were staying at an extremely remote cloud forest lodge when I had my first and only ghost experience. Something seemed off about that place, and not just the fact that all the rooms had twin beds. Sometime in the middle of the first night, I was woken by freezing cold air along my back and a force pulling my shoulder back and almost dragging me out of bed.

As I came to, I sensed that it was the ghost of a young teenage girl pulling on me because I was in her bed. Don't ask me how I knew that I just did.

The force wouldn't stop, and I was about to fall backwards onto the tile floor when I hissed "AL-TO!!!", through gritted teeth. The force stopped immediately, and I rolled forward onto my face on the bed. Before I could recover, I could feel the girl crawl into bed behind me. It was like an invisible force pushed on to the bed and settled in for the night.

I was more scared than I have ever been in my life! Even nearly drowning didn't scare me as much as this ghost.

I scooted over towards the wall and laid dead still. After an unmeasurable amount of time, the icy chill I felt from the ghost was too much. Reaching down, I grabbed the extra blanket at my feet and pulled it up to my chin. I was literally too scared to even look back over my shoulder to make sure my new wife was safe!

There would be no sleeping. My front half was sweating while my back half was covered in goose bumps. It was similar to cold sweats you get when you have the flu. All I could do was go over in my head how we were going to check out in the morning and find somewhere else to go.

Looking at me, Jennifer scolded, "Are you doing any work today or taking a mental health day?"

It was a sad joke, in the eight years I had been running our business, I hadn't taken a vacation that wasn't traveling out of state to visit her family or my family.

"Yeah, yeah, I'm going to the dungeon." My fond name for the office in the basement.

CHAPTER 4

THE RABBIT HOLE OF ALTERNATE MEDIA

MARCH 24, 2002

I own and operate a business selling engineering field equipment; drones, GPS, laser scanners and such. It could be exciting, but the changes brought on by the Covid years had turned it more into a job and less of a passion. Luckily, my salesmen were down to earth guys that knew the equipment first and how to sell it second.

I knew Ian, my Midwest sales guy, had spent years meditating, so I tried to innocently needle him for some information over one of our check-in video calls.

"Ian, you still meditating?"

"Every morning. If I don't my wife is going to take my meditation closet back and use it for her clothes," Ian chuckled. Ian was about ten years younger and shifted back and forth from a beard to clean shaven. He stayed fit and his bead bracelets always caught my attention. "I've found that meditation really helps me stay centered and chilled out," he continued, "especially with everything going on in the world. How's your meditation stuff going, boss?"

I grinned at his joke. "Interesting to say the least. Do you see things when you get deep?" Trying not to give up my hand.

"Ha, no. I just think about clouds or sitting in front of a waterfall. Then after about 20 minutes I feel relaxed, and I get up to walk the dog and get ready for work." Ian shrugged his shoulders. "Why, you see angels or something?"

I laughed heartily, "No man, just wondering how it is for you."

I had become obsessed with meditating since that galactic traveling episode. Initially, I had poked around the internet trying to find people that had experienced what I did that first time. It also renewed my interest in shows about the weird. To the point that I bought a subscription to the infamous channel for the woo-inclined, the Gaia Channel. Shows like Ancient Aliens and Finding Bigfoot on cable channels was no longer enough to quench my appetite for the weird.

"Well, you should try podcasts. Lots of metaphysical stuff out there if you are looking for different types of meditating." Ian shrugged again, "I usually focus on politics but sometimes meditation or spirit stuff pops up in my 'you should try this' feed. Just search like 'psychic' or something."

It was an interesting idea. I knew plenty of people that raved about podcasts, but I had never given the podcast world a chance. I couldn't watch the Gaia Channel while working, but I did listen to music all workday so podcasts should be perfect.

There are a lot of mid-level and low-level budget documentaries out there exploring everything from ghosts (probably the most popular), to ETs, to Bigfoot and monsters, to the Illuminati and everything in between. However, the real gold mine are podcasts. Compared to documentaries, podcasts cost a fraction of budget and time to make. Thus, everyone with a microphone in their basement seems to have a podcast these days.

The great part about all these folks is they do the research for you and then present it in audio and sometimes video format that they post to YouTube or Rumble. Many of these shows also do one better and interview 'experts' on particular subjects. An expert is usually someone with one to dozens of books on a particular subject. Some of my favorites are people that are not archaeologists but have studied alternative theories on various ancient culture around the world. Graham Hancock and his Netflix series *Ancient Apocalypse* and the History Channel's *Ancient Aliens* are two great examples.

CHAPTER 5

THE MEDITATION THAT CHANGED ME FOREVER

After months of meditating and expanding my mind with new documentaries and TV series about everything from ancient civilizations to UFO conspiracy theories beyond the Roswell crash, it was time to take my next step. A live metaphysical event.

I had signed up for two days of online meditations and channeling by a woman interviewed in a TV series about people that channeled higher beings and extraterrestrials.

Liza Tol, she channeled an extraterrestrial being from the Sirius star system that called himself Nomah.

Liza would channel this higher being from Sirius and lecture to the participants on ideas of consciousness, energy, frequency, and how Sirians can work singularly or as a collective consciousness. They also discussed sacred geometry, which has always fascinated me. I ate it all up, couldn't get enough. Liza also said that the Sirian entities would visit the attendees during our meditations to help us with our progression into better understanding consciousness.

It was also explained to us that beings from the Vega star system, were known as mystics. These beings delineated specific sounds that are the purest, like the 'OM' chant that is so popular in the Wooniverse here on Earth. Supposedly, sound can help humans raise their frequency, vibration, or density from our third density level to a higher density which is lighter. This follows the idea that higher density beings are purer and eventually transition to just light energy entities like angels. With God or Source or the Divine Being at the top of this tiered system.

Shifting the human body to the 4th or 5th Density seemed to be a big deal with the woo folks. It would supposedly release the pressure of 3D and would cause changes in the human body. Humans might feel their diet needed to change and yoga or qigong could help keep the body charged for spiritual work. I was also introduced to the ancient idea of chakras. All new to me, but something I would need to look into more in the future.

My first guided meditation with Liza was a little frustrating. I couldn't see anything in my head, or in my mind's eye. But I did get the sense there were five different beings in the room with me. Almost like shadows in my mind's eye.

My frustration would be short lived.

The final meditation of the workshop was used to call all the human attendees to a shared beach in our mind. We stood together on the beach and nine Sirian Masters from the 5th Density surrounded us. Three is an important number for the Sirians. Three Masters formed a triangle around the humans. Further out another three Masters formed a second triangle. Even further out from the second triangle, were the last three Masters forming a third triangle. Creating a circle around the largest triangle were other beings from the human attendee's spiritual teams. Every human in this group had come together, not by chance, but because we have all had some kind of contact with a group of extraterrestrials, extradimensionals, or light beings. It made sense to me.

If that revelation wasn't enough to blow my mind, the message I was about to receive during my meditation would change my life forever.

Pain was on both sides of the field. Humans on one side and blue-skinned Sirians on the other.

The Sirian's showed me their pain and it was immense. I could see myself as a female Sirian on Earth, it felt like it was ancient, ancient Egypt. I was a Sirian that had failed my human 'children'. I did not want to leave Earth. But I was forced to leave. I saw myself traveling through space. The pain of failure was unbearable. I was afraid for my 'children'. I was afraid I would never see them again.

Seeing all this in my mind's eye, I could also feel it. I physically cried during this meditation; literally sobbed from the emotional pain. Snot pouring from my nose and mixing with my tears. I couldn't move or wipe the tears.

But eventually my Sirian self-accepted that like a bird, I had to leave the land of winter and travel to the land of summer. The humans were entering a time of winter cycle that would span thousands of years. I knew I could not fail my 'children' the next time.

My Sirian self-plunged into my studies to make myself closer to Source. When I returned during the spring cycle of the Earth, I would be a higher density being and closer to Source and that would allow me to succeed in advancing my 'children' where I had failed before.

Now, in this time of humans, it is spring, and we have returned to the land of our 'children'.

My current human body resonates with the pain of leaving....

This experience really blew my mind. It was an amazing experience that opened me up to contact of a sort with other entities through consciousness contact. It had to be similar to the way some religious people believe they have prayed and met angels or even their god. Only in this experience I met ETs. Well, many people would argue that angels are ETs.

CHAPTER 6

ASSISTANCE WITHOUT INTERFERENCE

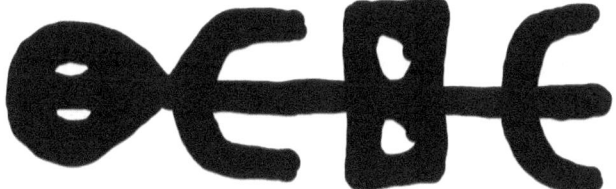

APRIL 10, 2022

That meditation nearly broke me. Liza disbanded the group for a good thirty minutes so everyone could recover.

When we came back together, she continued to channel her Sirian contact. The information provided was different than human history books, but it resonated in my chest. Resonated with my soul and I had no doubt it was the truth. Or at least true on some level.

Much later I would come to understand the idea of multiple timelines or the multiverse where there are an untold number of different copies of our universe playing out in their own way. Different timelines have different truths. It is possible that on another timeline, Hitler was killed in a bar fight as a young man and World War II never happened. Which begs the question, would that timeline be a drastically different world in 2022 than the world we live in? Or would some other German rise to force a World War II like the one our timeline experienced?

Liza's contact stated that Sirians tried to save humanity. They could see that humanity was heading for another cultural reset and for right or wrong, the Sirians felt they had to force humans to awaken. Once that effort failed and the Sirians realized it was wrong to force another race of beings to do anything, they knew they had to leave Earth.

Assistance without interference.

When some Sirians agreed to remain on Earth, they all agreed to help humans without directly interfering. These Sirians retreated to remote areas in the mountains and under the sea. No human could approach these 5th Density beings directly. These beings became hermits that devoted themselves to remotely serving humans that sought help. They acted like human Wi-Fi hotspots. Humans that could tune into the Sirian Masters could receive transmissions in the form of channeling.

Assist but not interfere.

The sense of abandonment that humans felt became a Species Wound. Unhealed energy from the abandonment must be healed. Self-blame, abandonment, these wounds come up as a pain or fear band within humans. We must get in touch with this large pain that has kept us separated from the beings we called gods during the abandonment times.

The channeled information claimed that if you feel into the darkness that is within, you can pop yourself through the pain/fear gap separating you from connecting with your Higher Self. Separating you from your spirit team that agreed to help you in this life.

This makes a lot of sense. Assistance without interference, unless requested. Many spiritual people will say that your team of spirits here to assist you in this life sort of have their hands tied. If you don't request help from your spirit team, then they can't give it.

The channeled being said working with abandonment issues in one lifetime lessens the pain in later lifetimes. Aches and pains, arthritis, stomach issues, lower back problems; these are the body trying to communicate the trauma to your current incarnation that has forgotten. The body is a translation mechanism.

Anxiety: pay attention to it and work with it as if it is a messenger.

Earth and humans have been moving through 26,000-year cycles of progression, downfall, and rebirth. Starting around the years 2010 and 2011, a new cycle has begun. Moving into the Age of Aquarius man is ready to heal its species wound and reconnect with the stars. Now 5th Density Sirian energy is communicating a little more directly with mankind. We have seen more people begin to channel, more light workers have appeared to heal without modern medicine, people are experiencing contact with other beings in their dream state, meditation more easily connects to other worlds and past life memories, and people are seeing literal Unidentified Flying Objects all over the world on a daily basis. Energies are becoming more open in areas all over the planet. Orange light balls in the sky are communicating with humans from a distance so not to frighten us.

A few years later, I did an Akashic Reading session and got some interesting and seemingly relevant information.

"Okay, I'm seeing Sirius. So Sirian energy. Thank you for sharing this because this is interesting for me to see in your energy and your records," said the Reader.

"So, Sirius is where now there is a line being drawn from Sirius to Earth. And I'm being shown, and there is a lot. Okay there is a lot of energy coming through. They are saying please believe this because there is so much energy coming through it might be mind-blowing. But I keep hearing, trust us, trust us, trust us. So, I'm showing you, like, being in this Sirius star system and coming to Earth. You landed on Earth before all your Earth lifetimes as a being from Sirius. This…is…okay, they're talking about this had both…if we are speaking in dualistic terms, you had both good and bad intentions. Overall good intentions, but there were some accidental things that happened. Let me see if they will expand on what they are trying to get across."

"You were supposed to get in and out, I guess, but there was a group of you guys that stayed here longer…than originally planned. You were supposed to help stop something from occurring. And that didn't happen. And if we go deeper into that, we are going to start getting into DNA manipulation and other entities. But basically, the important thing that they want to share…is that somewhere deep in the soul there is kind of like this…I don't know if I want to call it…not like blame, but just like, maybe feeling like you are not doing enough. Or didn't do enough in that lifetime. And they are saying that that wound is much, much deeper."

I interrupted her flow, "Can you tell if I was female in that life?"

"Gender…"

"I mean it's okay if you can't pick that up," I added.

"Yeah, they are expanding beyond that. Okay, so, yeah, I'm not sure about that particular life. But I can say what they are showing me is female pointing to Andromeda."

"Okay".

"Okay, yeah, I feel…I'm just going to leave that. I don't want to share information that is not coming through clear on my channel."

"Okay."

"But what they are showing me, for you, if you set intention around revisiting this lifetime that we are talking about right now. You will be able to get a 360-degree view by looking around. By going right back to where you are. Definitely feeling like there is some, there is some area by Egypt. Maybe what we would call Mesopotamia. Um, all around that particular area. But they are talking about three different areas. So, you did come here multiple times, this is just one of them that they are referencing."

"Multiple times from Sirius?" I asked for clarification.

She nodded her head. "And, yes, and other places. I'm getting, so more specifically, I'm getting two mains, um, and there may be more, but I'm only being shown two main lives from these records that we will call landings. And they are also mentioning Sirius B. So, this is where they are getting into connection, and this might be something that you know from this Earth lifetime because it's out there. But the Dogon Tribe that knew of Sirius B before the scientists did because the Sirians came and taught them this knowledge. So, there seems to be a connection with that, but they are not really going deeply into it. Um, but they are saying two main connections from Sirius and across the cosmos. And they are saying that more is going to come later to be paired with certain points on your journey. But I will say that they are saying two from Sirius, two from Arcturus…um feels like more than a few from Andromeda. Um, because galactically speaking, this is across millions, potentially even billions of Earth years."

Corroboration

The scientist in me will never leave. Finding corroboration for a past life as a Sirian that came to Earth in the past from two different sources is how I have traversed this Spiritual Awakening.

CHAPTER 7

MY SPIRIT TEAM?

JUNE 19, 2022

After that powerful meditation and connection to Sirian energy, I became obsessed with learning everything I could about myself, my past lives, my spirit guides, extraterrestrials, inner earth beings, Bigfoot, Dogmen, the quantum, **EVERYTHING**.

I found a psychic that offered a beginner's class to help people connect to their spirit guides. I've since come to prefer calling them our spirit teams. No entity is above or more worthy than another entity. My first meditation showed me that we are all One, be us human, tree, ant, angel, or Wookie from *Star Wars*.

The spirit team connection course started with a meditation to meet three spirits here to help you in this life. The exercise was to choose three ways that I wanted to feel in the future.

Given my life at the time, that was easy:

- *No Anxiety*
- *No Physical Pain*
- *Happy*

The psychic's guided meditation was beautiful, and a lot calmer than that first universe meditation!

I was guided in my mind's eye to a beautiful forest. In the distance was the sound of running water and I was to find my way to it. It was a gentle waterfall. I was to sit under it. Imagining the water as warm honey, it fell over me and coated my body in protection. The warmth filled my head and flowed down to my heart, down my arms, and through my legs to my feet. Now I was to welcome three spirits from my team; each with a solution for the three ways I wanted to feel in the future.

First, I saw a beautiful blonde man that could only be an angel. Dressed in Romanesque leather armor and white flowing fabric, with blonde curly hair. This being reached out and handed me a…. stick? What the hell? Why is he giving me a stick?

Oh well, no time to dwell. The meditation guided me to my second spirit. This was an odd looking human. White male, thin wispy white hair with a youthful face and overly large human eyes. I heard the word "Essassani" in my head. I would later learn that was a group of beings that people believe are hybrids between Earth Humans and the little grey extraterrestrials from Zeta Reticuli.

This Essasani handed me an Egyptian Ankh. Huh…cool, I guess. I would have to research it because despite the fact I had seen ankh's hundreds of times in photos and documentaries, I didn't actually know what it meant or was supposed to do.

Lastly, my final spirit stepped forward. This was a shock. The entity was a dark blue extraterrestrial with black eyes and an enlarged head. But instead of a goofy skintight spacesuit, this being wore flowing robes, like a Jedi. In my head I heard "Ascended Master". The being reached forward with his right hand and floating above his palm was a light emerald, green glow. Green was what this Ascended Master was giving me.

And just like that, it was over and my eyes fluttered open.

Green. I felt like that was supposed to help with my anxiety. In my youth my mother had taught me when I felt unsafe to imagine a yellow glowing cocoon of energy around me and it would protect me. I felt like I needed to change that color to green to help when I had an anxiety flare up.

The ankh was easy to research. My takeaway from it all was that the ankh is the union of the female and male genitalia; the union of Heaven and Earth. It represents eternal life and acts as the key to the gates of death and what lies beyond. One theory is that holding it preserves immortality. Which isn't a bad theory since all the pharaohs and gods in Egyptian hieroglyphs are always holding an ankh.

The stick? Seriously, what am I supposed to do with a stick? If it was a sword then I would think it was for protection or something. A stick I can only think is maybe a wand. What would I need a wand for?

Years later I would realize that the color green was not to help with my anxiety. That, I believe spirit was showing me that I needed to open my heart and do my inner work. The green was the color of the heart chakra.

For the stick, I have received a lot of evidence that it refers to some kind of healing device. Many historical accounts of the ancient gods (or ETs), told of a wand like device they had that could heal people or levitate objects. Given all my health issues, I believe this somehow symbolized that I would someday find a way to heal my physical ailments. That remains to be seen at the time of this writing.

The ankh is very interesting. A year after this meditation, I would end up on a surprise last minute trip to Egypt. Was seeing the ankh a heads up that I was going to Egypt where I would experience many spiritual downloads of information and spiritual upgrades? To this day, much like the stick, I am not sure what it was meant to tell me.

CHAPTER 8

PAST LIFE REGRESSION

SEPTEMBER 8, 2022

I need to preface the beginning of past life regression experiences by saying that I have always felt like I would die young. In my teens I didn't think I would live past 35. When I got to my early thirties, I began to think I wouldn't live past 40. After 40, I began to think, "damn, maybe I'm here for the long haul?"

My mother was always open minded and accepting of other people and their views. I knew she had done a little bit of psychic stuff in the late 1980's and early 1990's. One psychic she waited for 2 years to have a session with had told her that I was an Experiencer, because that's what mom's do. They get themselves a psychic reading and ask about their family.

The psychic said I was meant to experience the world, and I was a very old soul. I had heard the story but never thought much of it. I had

had other older people call me an old soul, so having a psychic parrot that same idea didn't mean much at that time. When I started telling my mom about my recent experiences, she was quick to recommend an online past life regression with a practitioner that she liked. It was easy for me to hop on to the Woo Train at this stage of my life; 20 years earlier and I would have shrugged my shoulders and taken the dog for a walk.

A couple days later I logged into the Past Life Regression session and went through the host's steps to access the past life. Calm, breathe, listen to her voice, and then find your spirit guide for this lesson and walk through a tunnel and into my past life.

After leaving the tunnel, I left my Spirit Guide behind. One last look reminded me that this was the blue non-human that seemed to be a main guide of mine. He was really tall with solid black eyes and a larger bald head, wearing white robes like my own personal cross between Obi Wan Kenobi and Yoda.

Leaving the tunnel, I looked down at my feet. I was wearing sandals on my little feet. Definitely not adult feet, maybe around eight years old. The sandals looked very Roman, simple with straps.

As the mist around me lifted, I could see that I was wearing Roman-style clothing like the one-piece tunic skirt outfit with gold colored embroidery on the edges of the clothes and a gold-colored cloth belt.

The surrounding area was overgrown with dead grass and scattered oak trees on rolling hills. I felt lost. I was the only person around. This seemed like a placeholder, so I told myself to move forward to my twenties when something important was happening.

The scene changed and I was around twenty, with dark curly hair and a fit body from hard activity. I somehow knew I was from a family that had wealth. I had been given the choice as that young boy to go into study with philosophers and become a teacher, or I could become a soldier. It appeared I had made the unfortunate choice of becoming a soldier.

I saw myself in battle gear of that era, surrounded by men fighting and screaming and dying. The world was a chaotic whirl of human flesh, hard metal, and brown horse fur. I was riding in a chariot, violently being shaken up and down. Side to side. Struggling to hold the reins with one hand, my spear with the other.

Before I can really comprehend what is happening, this world turns to black before flashing back into living color.

I'm finished.

The chariot has crashed, and I've fallen under it. The horse's anxiety from the chaos caused it to act in opposition to its training and we crashed. Taking in my surroundings, I see that I have been ripped in half at my waist! My torso is destroyed, and I don't even know where my legs have gone.

As I lay dying, choking on my blood, I wished that I had gone to school instead of plying the trade of war.

In my current life, I suddenly realize that this explains why I have NEVER trusted horses. It also makes sense why I have always been anti-war, military, police, anyone that tries to lord themselves over another through force and weapons. This soul memory may be why I worked so hard to get a higher education in my current life. I prided myself on being the first in my family to finish college. I worked my way through school, sadly taking 8 years to get a Bachelor's Degree. Eventually, I would finish with a Master of Science and a lot of student loan debt.

The interesting thing this Practitioner mentioned before the regression was that we could change the life we were shown. If we didn't like the way that life turned out, we could rewind it to the key moment and imagine ourselves taking a different path and then roll it forward to see how things change.

So, I tried.

I imagined myself rewinding that life as a Roman soldier back to when I first appeared as an eight-year-old boy.

It seemed to work. I was that boy again, only this time I chose the path of education, pen feathers and reading by candlelight. I saw myself attending school and then later as an older man, sitting in a room of philosophers. At a much older age, I was a teacher of young men. I saw that incarnation living a full life.

Lastly, I saw myself old, with a massive white beard lying in bed. My life wound down. This time I was surrounded by my children and grandchildren. A full life stolen from the mud and blood and guts of the battlefield.

This was the first and only time during a regression that I tried to rewind that life and choose a different path at a key timeframe. Thinking about this now, it forces me to consider the theory that there are an untold number of realities out there. Some people within the quantum field of science, and the metaphysical world, believe that every time a person makes a decision, there is break in the timeline and it splinters into two separate realities. One timeline is the one we find ourselves on based on our decisions. Then another timeline spins off following the other option that our current self-did not choose.

Yeah, it makes my brain hurt to consider the full scope of how the universe may work.

CHAPTER 9

CONSCIOUSNESS

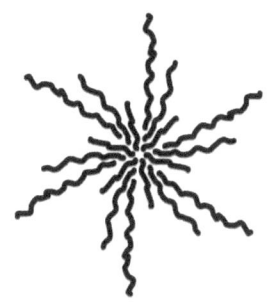

NOVEMBER 11, 2022

At this point, I am all in on the metaphysical. Or the 'Woo Woo', as detractors tried to label it. Spiritual folks said, yeah, the 'Woo', we can own that. Funny when an insult is grabbed by the insulted and embraced to the point that the insult loses its power.

Through a lot of reading, videos, and online courses, I had absorbed a workable understanding of consciousness.

Consciousness applies to all sentient beings; Humans, Extra-Terrestrials (ET), and Extradimensionals (ED). To be fair, some would argue everything from plants to fish to bugs to rocks have consciousness. I'm not one to argue against that idea, but I will stick to "higher" levels of consciousness as I understand.

The states of consciousness include Waking, Sleeping, Dreaming, and Meditation. Dreaming includes lucid dreams and precognition.

Meditation is the unbound pure consciousness and easier to access than your dreams. Meditation is also obviously easier to pull off than a physical encounter with ETs or EDs. Meditation would continue to change my worldview as the months and years plodded on.

Sometimes when you look into the dark with your consciousness, the dark looks back.

With all the podcasts I was consuming, I had found the mystery of Dogman to be fascinating. If you are new to the idea of Dogman, just imagine the evil wolf version of Bigfoot. The legendary Beast of Bray Road was a Dogman first described back in the 1980's along a lonely stretch of road in Wisconsin.

But unlike the mixture of good or scary reports of Sasquatch encounters, I have only heard horrific tales of Dogman encounters. It seems almost like the Dogmen are feeding off the fear of the humans they stumble across. A common theme is that the Dogman chases the storyteller but never captures them. Even though it would be easy to run the human down and eat them for dinner.

At one point, I was so focused on Dogman stories, that I believe I might have lit myself up to the consciousness of the Dogman. I believe this because there was a week of time where I could feel an entity watching me from the woods.

Every time I left my house and drove past a patch of woods; I could feel the intense gaze of an entity of some sort watching me from the tree line. I have felt being watched before, but that week felt much more focused.

Then I would drive past homes and shopping centers and feel nothing. A few miles later when I pulled parallel to another patch of woods, I could feel the same entity watching me again. Like that being could portal jump from the safety of one wood patch to the next as it followed me.

Needless to say, it was more than a little unnerving. Magnified by the large patch of woods across the street from our home and another twelve acres of woods behind our property.

I stopped listening to Dogman podcasts and stopped thinking about the beast. Immediately, the watching entity stopped.

Since this, I have come to learn that Dogman seems to have a very strong spiritual component to it. Much more so than Bigfoot seems to have. Others have commented that when they were thinking about Dogman a lot, or even trying to remote view the beast, the beast seemed to look back at them from the dark. This boogieman seems to be able to notice people focusing their attention on them and sniff them out.

Learning that, just makes me shutdown any ideas I may have of listening to stories about this incredibly mysterious and dangerous creature.

Fast forward in time and I'm working with a friend that is honing her skills with the QHHT practice. We were doing abbreviated sessions where she would count me down and do one life regression and then count me back up.

One of these occasions blew both our minds as I regressed back to a time on Earth around 1.5 million years ago. The evidence for that rough time frame is mind-blowing, but I'll get to that.

"Now you are coming down from your cloud, drifting and floating, coming down to the ground." Kristy cooed hypnotically. "Now, what do you see?"

"Hmmm, rolling hills with lots of big animals," I said.

"What do the animals look like?"

"They are huge and hairy…Wooly mammoths and wooly rhinos and looks like deer or gazelles. Saber-toothed cats are enemy."

"Oh, okay," Kristy began. "Can you look down at your body? What do your feet look like?"

"Hairy. Dog feet."

"Dog feet?" Kristy's voice quickened with excitement. "Can you look up your legs at your body and see what your body looks like?"

"Hmmmm, animal. I look like a wolf. Like a massive wolf bigger than any man."

"Are you walking on four legs or two?"

"We can stand on our hind legs when we interact with each other, like men do. But when we hunt, we get down on all four legs so we can chase down prey. The others with me look like werewolves," I said matter of fact.

"Do you have hands or four feet?"

"Looking at my hands, they are different than my feet. More like, hmmmm, like raccoon hands with really long fingers and nails. Mean, ugly raccoon hands."

"You said there are others with you?"

"Yeah. My tribe."

"Are they male and female? How many are there?" Kristy asked.

"Hmmmm, we are all male. Me plus five others. We are about ten feet tall when we stand up. Very muscular, large upper body, wide shoulders, big teeth."

"Are you on Earth?" Kristy asked.

"Yeah, but we used to live inside."

"Inside? You mean inner Earth?"

"Hmmm, yeah," I answered.

"Why do you live outside now?"

"We found a way out of underground. Underground was hard life. Not much food and many of my kind."

"Okay, so your group of Dogmen left Inner Earth to come outside. Can you go to the place you left Inner Earth? What does the entrance to Inner Earth look like?"

"Hmmm, it is on the side of a hill. Looks like cave opening but it has square stones like bricks lining the hole. Someone had to make it."

"What did you eat when you lived underground? Was there light underground? How did you see?" Kristy asked.

"Rats and lizards. We ate little things…"

"What about light?" Kristy asked again. "How did you see underground?"

"Some of the rocks made light. It was dim but you could see. My group was small, and we had no female so we had to be careful of the bigger packs. One day we found a new tunnel that took us up to the sky land. It was warm and bright and had so much food everywhere."

"Are you the pack leader?"

"No," I said. "The pack leader is the biggest of us. He is white and gray, mostly white. But two others challenge him a lot."

"Do you see any animals that walk on two legs? Not like you but any other animals?"

"Hmm, yes. Very small creatures with a little hair on body. They are dumb. My tribe can talk with our brains, but the little creatures cannot."

"Talk with your brain? You mean use telepathy?" Kristy asked, surprised.

"Yeah, but we have to look in each other's eyes to send mind speak. We talk that way and it is helpful when we hunt."

"Okay. Let us move forward to an important day in this life. Something important. What do you see?"

"Hmm, another pack like us. Another pack has found the way out and entered our valley. Hmm, thirteen of them and they have a female. Any pack with a female is strong. Stronger than us."

"What happens next?" Kristy asked.

"I want to run. This land is huge. But Leader wants to stay and fight for this valley. Two gang up on the Leader and defeat him. He ran away. Now new leader is gray. He tells us we will run to next valley over the mountains."

"Okay. Now let us move forward to the last day of this life as a Dogman. Where are you? What is happening?"

"Hmm, I am alone. My pack was slowly killed by the other pack with the female."

"What is happening?" Kristy prodded.

"I am fighting a wooly mammoth by myself."

"That sounds dangerous," Kristy said.

"Yes. Normally four or five of us can take one down but very dangerous for just me. It is like a small meadow surrounded by big trees. Oh, it hit me and I flew into a large rock."

"Are you okay?" Kristy asked.

"No. I think my back is broken. I can't move. The mammoth walks away. I just lay here and slowly die."

"You don't have to feel any pain; you are just an observer." Kristy said. "Looking at this life, why do you think you were shown this? What is the lesson of this life?"

"Hmm. To remind Matt that the universe is more varied and magical than any human realizes."

In my life now, I have had 3 back surgeries for herniated lumbar discs. The first at 35-years-old and the third at 45. I just find it interesting that my Higher Self would show me a life where I died from a broken back. Maybe there truly is something to the idea that past life problems and health issues manifest again and again in later life incarnations.

CHAPTER 10

SPIRIT COMMAND CENTER

JANUARY 13, 2023

One idea I came across in my searching is the idea of a Spirit Command Center. This is a location in the astral that only your spirit team has access. This is where your spirits and guardian angels can be met and interacted with safely. Personally, I cannot hear my team speak to me when I visit this safe place. But I have used this as a jumping off place for some cool consciousness projections, or astral projections.

This was my experience, but everyone will differ greatly.

First you need to connect to your Higher Self. I knew that my Higher Self could be represented as a candle, so I focused on that. Initially, I thought it was just a white candle with a yellow flame. But as I focused on the candle, it morphed and became clearer. The flame was light green and purple. It reminded me of fluorite crystals.

Next, the lesson told me to leave my human body sitting in my house and see my astral self-exit my body encased in a golden bubble of safety and warmth. My golden bubble exited my chest and flew up into the sky. I could see myself traveling in my bubble through the air until I reached a magical land of vivid colors. The landscape consisted of rolling hills of green grass surrounded by forests with tall mountains in the distance. A clear, cold stream meandered through the green rolling hills. In the distance stood a tall building like I had never seen before.

The building was more like a massive piece of white coral. The walls were organic with scattered openings that I assumed were windows of some kind. The entry at ground level was a massive, beautiful oak double door. Tall, with swirls of age and varying shades of brown. Two large, beaten iron rings hung from each of the doors.

Entering the coral castle, I realized I was wearing robes of the most beautiful vivid blue with a golden sash for a belt. The inside of the dwelling was a single long hallway. There were two or three stories on the inside forming a vaulted ceiling. Walls looked like white coral. Nothing was a ninety-degree angle. It was all organic. Windows were odd shapes and randomly placed and the doors were all massive. The center of the hall had many tables running the length of the hall. Oddly the tables were chest high and there were no chairs or stools. Each table had a different colored crystal ball in its center. There was a massive door at the far end of the hallway and a smaller sized door just to my right, near the entrance.

If things couldn't get any weirder, I realized this hall was populated by hooded beings. Each being was wearing either white or black robes with their hoods pulled up and hiding their visage.

Angels.

I don't know how I know but I just know. These are my Guardian Angels. I quickly counted the mysterious beings. Yep, sixteen. My seventeenth Guardian Angel is Jerome, he doesn't hide his visage like the others do.

I hadn't noticed him before, but my blue ET guide, my Ascended Master, was standing to my left and pointing at the door on my right. Turning, I could see the door had a large sign above it with my full name emblazoned. I reached out both hands and pushed the door open and stepped inside.

Whoa…

Upon entering, I was presented with a large table and many, many beings. There must have been 50, no maybe 100 beings in this room. But I could not see them all clearly, just the dozen or so closest to me. The one's further back shimmered like they were behind heat waves on a hot summer day. Some came to me, smiles on their faces, if they had faces, and seemed to greet me. I asked them their names, what they would guide me on, and how I could connect with them.

I swear if this dimension had crickets, I would have heard them.

I did not receive any answer, that I could tell from any of the entities. But I'll describe the ones that left their seats at the table and came to greet me.

The Angel from my earlier guided meditation to help with my anxiety. This Angel was a blonde male, with white clothes like you see in paintings from the Middle Ages. Next was the blue Ascended Master ET. The last one I was already familiar with was the Essassani.

A red-headed Mother Goddess type entity came to me. She was very large, like a giantess. Very beautiful with green eyes and matching robes.

A literal monster crab was next. I dubbed him Crabby. He was taller than me and had a shell that was dark blue mottled. I totally felt fine meeting him, but I suddenly felt like I didn't want to eat crab in the future. Like I was guilty to have ever eaten shellfish in my life.

Next a Gray Man came before me. Hard to tell what kind of being the Gray Man was. He was very tall and human looking, but he had a larger head than seemed normal for a human.

It is hard to describe the next being. It was literally a being of light, a Light Being. Just light. Mostly white but also rainbow coloring around the outer edge of its shape.

I swear my childhood made up the next entity on a whim. A very tall and burly humanoid wearing medieval clothing stepped up. It was humanoid in body, but its head was like that of a massive golden eagle. The being reminded me of a gryphon but with the body of a human instead of a lion. He seemed very jovial, somehow, considering his eagle beak seemed more threatening than comedic.

Last was probably the king of weird. On its surface, it was something many an Earthling would be familiar with, a praying mantis. Only this Mantid was eight feet tall!!!! The being was mostly green and had a golden cloth sash over its shoulders and draping down in front of its body like a big scarf.

I stood there staring at the entourage that had left the table to 'greet me'. No one moved or spoke. I guess that was all for today, so I felt myself rewind through the building, to the pastoral setting, to my golden bubble, to the sky and back into my house and body.

"What…the fuck…was that?"

CHAPTER 11

WHERE DID MY DREAMS GO?

JANUARY 17, 2023

I don't dream. I don't have nightmares, and I don't wake up remembering dreams.

I used to dream. When I was in my teens and twenties, I used to have nightmares and whacky dreams. Dreams about worlds that didn't exist. Dreams about being chased by monsters that didn't exist.

Sometimes black and white dreams. Sometimes color.

Around my early thirties, I seemed to have stopped dreaming. Or at least I don't wake in the night or even in the morning remembering any dream. Maybe the rigors of life and having children burned out my fuse and eliminated my dreams.

Then one night, something odd happened. Not a dream but odd. I had weird visions of little gray beings before I fell asleep. I was really restless that night.

At 2:56 am, I woke to a loud "Hello!" It ripped me from sleep, and I flew out of bed and went down the hallway to check on my kids before I was fully awake. But they were asleep. Returning to bed, my wife was also asleep.

"What the heck said 'Hello'?"

Lying there, I remembered the strange gray beings before I fell asleep. A tickle at my memory had me showing the gray beings hockey. Showing the rules of the game. Sending the feeling of cold to the beings. Then trying to explain that we play hockey because it's fun. For the life of the little guys, they couldn't understand why humans will choose to be cold for fun.

"Man, that was weird," I mumbled as I drifted back to sleep.

In a session with an Akashic Reader, she told me one of my past lives on another planet with 'monsters' gave me nightmares in this life. She was giving me a lot of information so that little nugget made it in the notes, and I forgot about it.

Since then, I've had time to reflect on what she said. In my teens I did indeed have a lot of nightmares where I was chased by impossible monsters. Creatures that never existed on our planet Earth. Or at least not in our fossil record.

Maybe those monsters were soul memories bleeding through from other lives? Slipping from the knowing of my Higher Self into my subconscious and manifesting as dreams?

CHAPTER 12

MY BEST IDEAS

JANUARY 21, 2023

Meditating can be tiring. Just depends on the type of meditation, length, and if the meditator goes really deep. By deep, I mean can you get to the Theta brain state just above sleep.

To get around the fatigue that some of my meditations cause, I have started to 'sit quietly'. Sit in my recliner, ground myself and breathe, and just focus on blanking my mind and seeing what comes. If I am having a difficult time with that, I will imagine myself sitting in an empty movie theater before a movie starts. It's dim and the screen is just a massive blank slate. For me, the screen is gray. But I recommend going with what feels right for you. Maybe it is a white or black screen.

It is a great method for listening to your Higher Self or even just the universe. Many great minds have used a similar method from Einstein, to Edison, to Tesla. In fact, Thomas Edison would sit in a chair with his arms on the armrest. He had a ball in each hand. If he fell asleep, he would drop the balls and wake from the clatter. His goal was to get just to the point of falling asleep to get inspiration. Today, we would say he was trying to get to Theta and stay there without going all the way to sleep. Heck, even the Scientific American magazine wrote an article on this in 2021.

Working from home afforded me the ability to meditate or sit quiet after lunch. One day while quietly sitting in my recliner, focused on nothing, I suddenly realized that I get my best ideas while driving or standing in the shower. Something repetitive.

For instance, when I was at a bad spot in my career, I was driving an 8-hour route from a job back to my home in Oregon. It was a lonely drive through the mountains. Highway speeds along curvy roads, surrounded by mountain peaks and eighty-foot-tall conifers.

Suddenly out of nowhere, I had the idea to create a business that rented iPads for field survey work. It was like a lightning bolt to my cerebellum.

Put the iPad in a waterproof case, get cellular service, spare battery and a carrying strap and bam! The birth of an entirely new industry that didn't exist at that time. I ended up running with it and am now in our eleventh year of business.

Another time, I was driving after dark, in a rainstorm. Something in my head yelled, "look to the right, an elf!".

What?!

I looked to the right and it was a parking lot. Weird, where did that voice come from?

A quarter of a mile later, a wet, bedraggled mockingbird flew past the headlights of my car.

Okay, wait a minute. I'm a trained ornithologist and I know that songbirds are not going to be flying around at night unless it's migration. If it was migration, the birds would be hundreds to thousands of feet in the air. But mockingbirds don't migrate and this is winter. Plus, birds tend to hunker down when it's raining this hard.

Did an elf just past the front of my car in the form of a mockingbird? Or since I have never seen an elf, did my brain just interpret what I saw as a mockingbird?

There is definitely something to the variety of meditations that people find useful. Full on meditation, sitting quietly, or moving. Another example of moving is called labyrinth walking. This is where the practitioner walks a maze slowly and methodically. Allowing your mind to wander and bring you information from the universe.

Along this line is doing repetitive actions. Washing the dishes or folding laundry. Something that is 'mindless'. An action that is repetitive and takes little brain power to do. That allows your brain to connect with the universe or Source and pull in ideas.

CHAPTER 13

PYRAMID DOWNLOAD

At the time, I did not know that many people on our planet have received a pyramid download.

A download is when a sudden idea of a device, story for a book, or healing modality pops in your head. Usually, it takes place during a Theta brain state in the recipient. The brain can dip into Theta during meditation, or repetitive activity like washing dishes, driving on the freeway, or taking a shower.

My download came during a meditation.

I have seen many, many pyramids during meditations. But this was different. I saw the large Giza pyramid of Egypt, new and shiny with a gold-colored cap and bright white sides. The smooth sides were likely polished limestone given the material available in the region. Even though the capstone was gold in color, I somehow sensed it was a massive piece of quartz that was encased in gold leaf.

Energy.

I had the strong feeling that the Giza pyramid was an ancient source of free energy. Unfortunately, it no longer works because the Nile has changed course and pulled away from the front of the pyramid. Not to mention the fact that its functionality has been destroyed with the removal of the capstone and what appears to have been metal wires in the narrow shafts above the King's Chamber. Remember, quartz can release electricity through piezoelectric function and powers many of our modern devices. Gold is a wonderful transducer of energy and that's why high-end plugs like speaker cable plugs are gold plated. There is a lot of theories about how the Giza pyramid created power and there are numerous books on this that seem plausible to me.

One of the early researchers in this area was Christopher Dunn. He hypothesized that the Giza pyramid was a chemical power plant.

I got the impression that pyramid power needed to be returned to the world.

I remembered seeing copper tube meditation pyramids. Big enough for the user to sit inside of the pyramid shape. But just as that popped in my head, I got the message that the pyramids on Etsy were wrong. For one thing, they had straight sides. The Giza pyramid has bent sides, but the bend is so small that you can't see it unless you view the pyramid from the air. The Giza pyramid is an eight-sided pyramid, not four.

The other massive error with the meditation pyramids today's humans were 'promoting' is the fact they lack solid sides. This was a big impression from my download. The sides of the pyramid help guide Earth energy from the ground and causes it to swirl into a vortex in the interior. Big at the base, small at the top. Just like an inverted tornado of energy.

But that wasn't all. I was shown a copper tube pyramid with crystals inside and epoxy to squeeze the crystal and release piezoelectric energy. Then the outer walls of the pyramid to help encase the Earth energy.

This would mimic many aspects of the Giza pyramid. Not the massive amounts of energy generation, but enough energy generation and focus to help a person spending time in this meditation pyramid. Healing, physical energizing, and communication with your Higher Self or higher vibrational entities.

Maybe one of the ancient pyramids was used to open communication pathways from humans to aliens.

Later, during my first QHHT session, my Higher Self would hammer home the idea that meditation pyramids need to have solid sides. That pyramids are healing devices and communication devices with the universe.

CHAPTER 14

DRAGONS ARE REAL

JANUARY 28, 2023

Some days I get the feeling I need to meditate. Sometimes it comes in the form of my anxiety ratcheting up. Sometimes I just feel spirit has a message.

On one of those days, I felt the need to be silent.

In my afternoon meditation, my astral body popped out of my physical body. My consciousness or astral body was just floating a few hundred feet above my house. Not knowing what to do next, I suddenly had the desire to check in on my aging parents in California. In the blink of an eye, I zipped across the United States to the farmland of central California. But before I could track down my parent's house, I felt pulled North. Hard. Like the heavy pull of an ocean rip current.

Having spent time on Mount Shasta twenty years prior, I instantly recognized the mountain and the general area. I floated over to Black

Butte on the west side of Mount Shasta. It is an oddly evenly shaped cone of black lava rock. As I came around the small mountain, I took notice of the space between Mount Shastina and Mount Shasta. Mount Shastina is this weird little sister mountain growing out of the larger Mount Shasta. Right where they merged on the south side. Something was drawing me to that area, and I zeroed in like a bee to clover flowers.

Floating towards that area, I instantly found myself inside a cave. I don't remember the transition from exterior to interior, but here I was. The inside was wide and wound down into the mountain more like a tunnel than a natural cave. It felt like the rock tunnel went on forever.

When the tunnel finally ended, it opened into a massive, and I mean massive, cavern. There was light piercing every nook and cranny. Alien housing structures were everywhere. It appeared to be some kind of city, underground city. The people were very foreign. Humanoid looking but odd at the same time. Very tall with tan skin and wearing robes.

Gawking at the sight, I failed to see the tall female local approach me. I blinked at her. She was human-looking but very tall and slender and her face was almost elf-like with larger almond shaped eyes and wearing flowing robes. She smiled and telepathically spoke into my mind, "It is not time for you to be here."

She somehow touched my astral form. With her hand squarely on my chest, she pushed me backwards. Backwards into the rock wall!

I found myself inside a different, much smaller cavern. Whereas the last cave seemed manufactured, this was natural. Stalactites and stalagmites were everywhere, and the floor was smooth but undulated from the vagaries of nature.

Once I had my bearings, I realized I was being watched by a dragon!!

At that moment, I knew what it felt like to be a mouse cornered by a house cat. I stood motionless and thought to myself, "Ah shit, I literally dropped into this guy's house."

The dragon was immense. Dark-colored but not completely black. Its belly scales were a little lighter than the rest of its body which had dark scales. These were black with a dark purple iridescence like you sometimes see on birds. Where the bird's feathers appear black but when the sun catches the bird right, the feathers carry a sheen to them, sometimes purple and sometimes a rainbow.

I was pretty much under the control of this mythical beast. If he wanted me to live, I'd live. If he wanted me dead, I had no doubt he could squash my little astral body. Strangely, I never felt threatened. Instead, I sat down with my legs crossed. Which at the time made me laugh because my physical body is so stiff I had long lost the ability to sit cross-legged on the ground.

The dragon cocked his head to one side, then turned his head to look at me with just one eye. The similarity to a cat's movements was uncanny. The mouse feeling hadn't left.

Like a shot, the dragon's head lunged towards me and stopped inches from my face.

"Snoof", he snorted heavily.

My long hair blew in the wind of his breath, but I did not move. The dragon slowly pulled his head back and seemed to grin at me. A sparkle in his large red eyes. I felt like I passed a test.

The dragon bent his body around to his right. When he returned to face me, he held a tiny marble between two of his talons on his front claw. Reaching his claw towards me, I was presented with what I realized was a large, light green crystal ball. The dragon was so massive the volleyball-sized crystal ball appeared as a marble in his clutches.

Looking into the dragon's mesmerizing eyes, I reached out my hand and touched the crystal with my index finger.

Poof!

I found myself standing before my blue ET guide. We were in the pastoral area outside my Spirit Command Center. My guide led me to the organic building and inside. He took me to one of the tables with a crystal ball at its center. He looked at me expectedly and I leaned my face down to the crystal.

Poof!

I was transported to a jungle. I was alone. I spun in a circle and chose a direction. No idea why that direction, but it felt right. It didn't take long before I walked out of the jungle and into an alien landscape. I stood at a long border between lush jungle and dry, reddish desert. Off in the distance I could see what appeared to be the Sphinx of Egypt. However, this Sphinx looked much newer than the iconic figure in today's Egypt.

Whoa!

My blue ET guide appeared standing next to me. Turning, he silently walked towards the Sphinx. Only now the Sphinx no longer had the head of a human, it was a cat. If I had to guess I would say it was the sculpture of a leopard, but definitely the Sphinx. I felt this must be what the Sphinx looked like before it was brutalized by the ego of an Egyptian Pharaoh.

The feeling this had something to do with my meditation pyramid was undeniable.

Once we stood before the Sphinx, an odd thing happened. Well, odd is a spectrum at this point.

The stony left front leg moved without crumbling! The stone beast lifted its left paw to reveal an opening in the ground. Standing before the opening, I could see there were descending steps into the darkness. I could feel cool air emanating from the opening. Looking at my guide, he just stared at the hole. I guess he's not going to lead the way.

I went down the stairs, followed closely by my ever-silent ET buddy.

At the bottom of the stairs was a corridor. Perfectly rectangular. Taller than wide. The walls were carved from the black and red granite of Egypt. I could see a light at the end of the corridor and followed it. The light was waiting inside a square room. This chamber was tall, maybe twenty to twenty-five feet tall. First to catch my attention was a square basin about thigh high. It reminded me of photos of the King's sarcophagus in the great pyramid. But this is where resemblances stopped. This basin was full of liquid metal. It must have been mercury.

The square basin had large black obelisks, maybe fifteen feet high at each corner for a total of four. That was small potatoes compared to what confronted me from behind the two obelisks furthest from me.

Two unnaturally tall beings stood motionless, watching my stunned visage. Each being was taller than the obelisks. One was a man with a falcon head, but not realistic, more like I was looking at a 3D representation of a wall painting of Horus. The other being was just as tall and stylized like the first. The second was a man with a black jackal head. Was this Anubis?

My brain was spinning.

These two gods of ancient Egypt were brothers. According to Egyptologists, Horus was the Egyptian god of healing and protection, the sun and the sky. Anubis was the protector of graves and the guide of the underworld.

Before I could do or think anything further, I was blasted back to my spirit hall. Almost groggy, I was guided back to the room filled with my spirit team. Seeing them gave me the feeling they are with me for support and always nearby.

I have always found Egypt interesting. I mean who doesn't think that the pyramids, Sphinx, and animal headed gods are interesting? With that being said, there are a lot of places in the world that I would want to visit before Egypt.

However, meditations are more often than not, showing me shadows of pyramids. Many take me to a seemingly older Egypt than we know now, where the Sphinx is alone and there are no pyramids around it.

Astral explorations of ancient Egypt will pop up again in the future.

CHAPTER 15

STAY GROUNDED

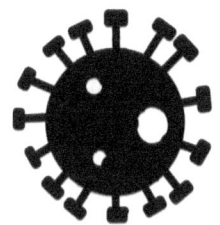

Matt and Jennifer sat silently in her cancer doctor's office.

I hate doctor's offices. Especially this office. My wife had battled breast cancer the year prior and undergone lumpectomy surgery. We expected an extremely low chance of cancer returning based on all the tests she had undergone and their results.

An elderly woman wrapped in a standard white lab coat entered and took a seat. "Hi guys, thanks for coming in today," said the doctor.

Jennifer gripped my hand stronger. "Well, let's not dance around it," I said monotonously.

"Yeah…As you know, we saw something in your 12-month post-op mammogram. So, we had you go for the MRI to get a better look. Let me pull it up here on the computer screen." She fumbled around with her mouse. Opening files, moving images around, then finally zooming in on what was obviously a breast. "Here is the tag we placed after the last surgery so we would know where we removed the tissue in that surgery. Here and here and here, you can see there are new nodules of cancer that were not there last year before your surgery."

I grasped my wife's hand a little harder. "I thought there was only a 5% chance of that cancer returning. So why are we here again 12 months later?"

"Well, I honestly don't understand it. I've never seen this before. I presented this in our weekly meeting with the breast cancer surgeons and no one in there has ever seen a cancer return in the same area like this. Not a short time later and not after all the tests showed such a low chance of reoccurrence."

"This is bullshit," Jennifer muttered. "I'm not going through this bullshit anymore. Take them off. Both breasts. Double mastectomy. I want this done so I can live my life."

What the fuck, man? What cruel joke is the universe playing here?

CHAPTER 16

COSMIC MESSAGES

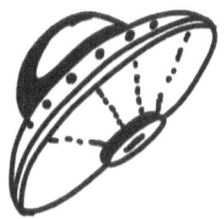

A few days after my wife got the brutal news that her breast cancer had returned, I settled down for a meditation. Nothing special happened this time. No astral travel or anything profound. But I had begun to pull four cards from the Galactic Heritage card set after any meditation that was, well, mundane. To do this, I would keep my eyes closed. Shuffle the deck and then spread it out on the table best I could. I would sit and feel where I was drawn in the pile. Slowly I would pull four cards and place them in a diamond shape in front of me.

This deck of Galactic Heritage cards are not tarot cards. They are the work of Liza Tohl and the ET entity she channels. The ET channeled the information on each card and explained how the cards can be laid out in four specific geometric shapes with different numbers of cards based on the type of information the user would like to pull from the universe.

It is a beautiful deck of 108 cards. They cover aspects of how you might be related to the Founders, Arcturus, Lyra, Vega, Pleiades, Sirius, Orion, and Zeta Reticuli.

The geometric layouts for the card fall into four groups: Star Lineage, Karmic Challenges, Higher Guidance, and Personal Questions.

On this day, I asked for Higher Guidance and laid out the cards. Opening my eyes, I saw that I had pulled the 71 card, Homing Beacon; 93 card, Assistance without Interference; 60 card, Coming Full Circle; and finally, the 81 card, Learning to Nurture.

Are you kidding me? If these cards didn't scream, "Here Do This Now", I don't know what would. They all seemed to be related to my wife.

Homing Beacon / Vega (*Future*) - Develop your ability to connect to Source or Higher Self. Okay, that makes sense. Doesn't everyone want to connect to Higher Self? Grab knowledge your smarter Higher Self might know?

Assistance Without Interference / Sirius (*Future*) - Assist someone in your life without interfering. So, I guess this means help Jennifer with her cancer journey but don't give my opinion? Let her choose everything and just quietly go along? Guess that makes sense. It is not my body or my choice. I'm just along for the ride.

Coming Full Circle / Sirius (*Present*) - Sirian's task to awaken humans is complete. Poised for a powerful life transformation. Well yeah, I guess a double mastectomy is about as "powerful a life transformation" a woman can undergo. Maybe even more so for a mother.

Learning to Nurture / Zeta Reticuli (*Present*) - Whoa…Yesterday Jennifer and I had aura photos taken. For me, it showed that I am lacking in self-care. This card seems to be saying the same. It literally reads; it is time to honor your self-nurturing needs without guilt. It also could mean it is my task to Nurture Jennifer through this life transformation.

Dang that was powerful. Three cards focused on my wife's current and future journeys and one card on my current journey. Makes sense that I would need to work on self-care without feeling guilty if I'm going to be there for my wife during these surgeries and five months of chemotherapy.

Successive days and card drawing only expounded on my personal growth.

74, Conduct ceremonies that express my sacredness.

13, Find your creative energy and release it.

55, Let go and follow the flow, even if you don't know where it is going.

103, Be truthful with self. Go deep within and open to seeing what you need to see for yourself highest good. For assistance call on Essassani Energy. Wait a minute, one of my first spirit team members I met was an Essassani that gave me the Egyptian Ankh!

86, Equality of all things is a universal principle. But we must first heal our fear of lack before we can fully embrace this principle.

104, May have to walk a solitary but authentic path. Again, the Essassani cards.

70, Complete Surrender, let go of the control and trust the universe to be as it needs to be. I am a bit of a control freak, to be honest.

37, Choose to remove focus from negative self-talk and use your ability instead for spiritual evolution. Dang that is profound.

95, Be a leader without ego. This hit home for me. I own two businesses and have multiple employees that I lead. It is a balancing act between being confident and not egotistical.

21, Take care of yourself as you would a precious gift, and then you can give more to others. Wow, profoundly strong words.

31, Examine how your linear thinking keeps you stuck.

16, A strong trait of the Lyran civilization is protectiveness. They were often like lions protecting their cubs when it came to protecting their offspring or territory. Thus, this trait can be helpful or obsessive. Yeah, this is me. I'm like a momma bear when it comes to protecting my children and my business. This card hits hard.

CHAPTER 17

THAT WAS NOT A DREAM

Everything going on in my life seemed to be unlocking the dream world again. Many times, they were dreams, without a doubt. However, sometimes these 'dreams' would wake me, and I just knew they were real. They didn't have the dreamlike state to them. Instead, these 'dreams' were so real I could recall all the details around me from the color of chairs to the texture of tables and walls, to the smells of the locations.

One of these 'dreams' stuck with me. I had never seen any movie like this dream, so I don't feel it was a movie scene infiltrating my sleeping mind.

Furthermore, this dream seemed unnaturally long. It spanned many days, and I even slept and woke and slept in this dream. I was in some sort of research program, but not just a research project, it had a military hospital feel to it. I was one of four subjects in this program. One female and the rest of us were male. We all wore light green hospital scrubs and were relegated to our own small room. The room had a cot-style bed, a small table and one chair. There was a sink and a toilet.

We were not allowed to leave the room. At regular intervals a nurse would enter the room with a red tray, like the ones from high school cafeterias. On the tray was four small white pill cups. Three of the cups were pills that acted as a food supplement, the last cup was a pill for the program. I don't know, but I got the feeling this pill would make us sleep and was supposed to help us unlock some kind of psychic abilities.

I'd take the four pills and lay down on the sparse little bed. I didn't even get under a sheet or sad excuse for a blanket. I would just go to sleep.

Then I would wake in my dream. There would be a new set of pills in their little white paper cups on the table. I took them and returned to sleep.

Then I woke again. Repeated the motions of pill popping and returned to sleep.

In my dream, it felt like I slept and woke for weeks. Finally, I woke for real. It was still dark, and nothing was amiss in my bedroom. Damn. I don't know what that was, but it was more a memory than a dream.

Dreams had eluded me for the last few decades. But all this inner work seemed to have restarted my dreaming. Sometimes it was fantastical, sometimes ho-hum, and sometimes it was downright scary. Many times, I would wake and forget the dream by the time I rolled over.

One restless night, I woke from dreams over and over again until morning. The first dream, I was fighting Freddy Krueger. It seemed to drag on forever as I fought him off, ran, got ambushed, fought him off again. Rinse and repeat. Then Batman appeared and started fighting Freddy. I took that opportunity to run and then I woke.

Then I had two strange dreams back-to-back. In both, my wife was unable to have kids. They were sad lives. We had each other but something was missing, and we knew it. In one of the lives, she also had to have a double mastectomy to combat cancer just as she was fighting that battle in this life.

Finally, I dreamt of my drinking problem. I was drinking so I wouldn't remember the things that happened in my sleep when I astral traveled.

I also began to remember things that had happened in my youth. In my teens, I would often wake up punching the wall that my bed was pushed up against. Or I would even swing at the air and roll out of my twin bed and hit the floor. Our bodies naturally suppress our muscles while we sleep so we don't hurt ourselves. So even at the time I thought it was weird. I also remember sometimes punching the wall and waking to see the streetlight in the front yard being way too bright. I even mentioned it to my mother recently when the memory returned, and she was shocked. Now that I brought it up, she also remembered sometimes waking and thinking the streetlight was brighter than usual.

Woke this morning more groggy than usual. I was dreaming about two different ET groups. I was with them at a big table. But I'm not sure what we were discussing. Not even sure what kind of ETs they were.

I had forgotten this, but eight years ago, on a lazy Sunday afternoon during the summer, I had the house to myself. It was warm and I was reading in the living room when I dozed off. I found myself in some other guy's body. Instead of summer it was autumn. I knew it was that time of year because of the wet wild grass smell that happens in September. The grass is dead, and an early morning dew creates a very specific smell.

The body that encased me was sitting in an oak Savannah woodland. The trees were spaced out and dead grass filled the voids between the trees. As soon as I was finished taking in my surroundings, I found myself with a shotgun in my hand. My boots were off, and my feet were barefoot. I put the barrel in my mouth, my big toe in the finger guard, and I kicked the trigger. Ending that life.

I snapped awake from that 'dream'. At the time I thought maybe a demon had tried to attack me. But now, a couple of years into this Awakening to the Wooniverse, I realize it could have been a spiritual attack, but given everything, I think it could have been one of my Soul Echoes. Did I somehow connect to that Soul Shard and see his death? Was it a past life?

I believe that we have a strong connection to other pieces of our soul. We are living our authentic life in the here and now, but we are only a piece or shard of our Oversoul.

I saw this in a meditation once. We have a large soul that is connected to many other Soul Shards. Like a cluster of crystals. It should be possible to connect to our other Soul Shards and see through their eyes as they live out their own authentic life.

With further introspection on this idea. I believe that many Channelers are tapping into their other self in another plane of existence. It seems to make sense. Your Higher Self won't do anything to hurt you. So, what if your Higher Self is sitting there playing a video game and you are the character? And your Higher Self has a gamer headset on with the microphone. When you channel your Higher Self hands the headset over to one of your other selves, our Soul Echoes that is a higher density and knows the game.

CHAPTER 18

THE PSYCHIC THAT BLEW MY MIND

MARCH 7, 2023

After all the bizarre stuff that had happened between meditations, astral traveling, and bizarre dreams, I figured it was time to have a session with a professional psychic.

There was a woman that I heard on a podcast that I really resonated with. Just so happened that angels and spirit guides were her specialty. Plus, she was good at helping people understand what their psychic strengths were so they could focus on developing those.

My session with Nelly Loyham finally arrived and to be honest, I was nervous as hell.

"Hi, so nice to meet you, Matt!" Nelly was a short blonde woman with way more presence and energy than a stature of that size should be able to contain.

"Great to meet you. I'm nervous and excited." I was being honest. I never thought I would ever voluntarily call up a psychic.

"Okay, no reason to be nervous. Now, have I ever worked with you before? Strange question, I know, but I am half in a trance when I do a session, so I don't remember everything, and I tend to forget the people I work with. Sorry in advance for that."

"No, this is our first time talking."

"Okay, cool. Well, let's hop right in. Is there something specific you want to talk about first?"

I went on to discuss my problems with my lower back, my three discectomy surgeries and all the sciatica pain I lived with. I discussed the weird sensation of waking at night, clenching my jaw and how that was new. She connected with her guides and discussed some of the things I could try. Then she went on to talk about my psychic abilities she was sensing.

The two abilities she sensed the strongest for me was Knowing and Feeling.

Knowing was strong for me. Ideas come to me easily. I knew things I shouldn't know, like premonitions.

According to Nelly, feeling could include three sub types: Emotion, Physical, and Esoteric. Emotion is when you can feel other people's emotions. Physical meant you could feel another person's health. And Esoteric is when you feel a gush of energy from another person. Nelly thought she sensed that I could feel Emotion and Esoteric. She told me I could learn to read other people like she was reading for me.

Well, that's great but I don't think that is for me!

She dubbed me a Super Empath for how strongly I could feel others' emotions. Afterwards, reading over my notes from this session, this made a LOT of sense. I hate crowds and prefer to be by myself. It is because I am an open conduit for the emotions of those around me. Luckily, Nelly taught me a prayer to recite before leaving the house every day.

"Archangel Michael, please place a shape shifting energy shield around me. Keep my energy inside the shield and block other energies from entering my shield." She said that Archangel Michael is the helper of all Light Workers and now I use this mantra or prayer religiously. My son is also a Super Empath and he uses this prayer.

We have also created the habit of visualizing an energy shield forming over our body to keep out the energy of others. I imagine the suiting up that Iron Man does. I envision putting on a spiritual power belt that sends an energy shield up and over my head and down and around my feet. Fully encased in spiritual protection. I'll visualize doing it four, five, maybe six times before walking into a store.

"Wow. Okay, can we look at my spirit guides now?" I asked. The anticipation was killing me.

"Hmmmm, yeah, wow, lots of energy there. You know, when I teach people to connect to their spirit team, I usually tell them to meditate and ask their team to take a few steps back and then come in one at a time. You have so many guides you need to ask them to back up like thirty feet from you and then meet them one at a time!" She laughed melodiously.

"Whoa, really?"

"Yeah, okay, let's start with your angels. Seventeen. You have seventeen angels, and your lead angel is named Jerome." She laughed again. "Jerome presents himself as an old guy with a monocle and he's really funny. You know, in all the years I've done this, I have never seen an angel wear glasses, especially not a monocle!"

I laughed at the idea of some old angel dude with a monocle like the rich guy on the Monopoly box.

"You know, you are a Light Worker," she said so matter-of-factly. "Most people have one to three guardian angels. Once you get over five or so, you have a divine mission in this life. This isn't an ego thing, it just is. When you set up this life incarnation, you decided to take on a mission beyond living the 3D life experience."

I laughed internally. Does this mean I'm like a spiritual mob boss?

"Let's look at some of these non-angel guides you have." She paused. "Yeah, interesting. You have an awful lot of entities in your spirit team, they appear to mostly be pioneers and adventurers. Reminds me of my team. For you, I see an ancient master like a Kung Fu master, a Shaman like from South America, an old-time explorer like a European in the unsettled lands of America and an ancient Native American woman. Now, she's interesting, she's coming forward and wants to talk. Give me a second." This piqued my interest as I was frantically taking notes. I stopped and looked up.

"Well, I've never had this happen before, but she just said she's Pocahontas. Well, that is a new one for me."

Surely it can't get any crazier than that, right! I was wrong.

"I'm not surprised but it isn't terribly common. Lots of people have an ET or two in their team, but you have lots and lots of ETs."

"What! What do they look like," I gasped.

"Well, there is one blue guy, big head, I get the Ascended Master feel." This had to be my main Blue ET buddy. "Then there are six that are the same, they are tall and slim, with long heads, and very scientific. Then I see a dragon, very large with a dark iridescent sheen to his scales, male. Ah, he said he loves you very, very much."

I grinned like the Cheshire Cat.

"You know, I've only seen this guide one other time. Only one other person I've met in twenty years of doing this that has a cyclops and that is me."

"What?" I stammered. "What does a cyclops look like?"

"Well, you can ask your spirit guides to look like whatever you want them to. But to me, the cyclops, both mine and yours, look like Chewbacca with one big eye. They are very defensive and protective. They are from the Middle Earth Realm where the other large creatures live like dragons and giants. The smaller creatures like that live in the Fairy Realm. You probably have more than a hundred guides, or at least close to one hundred."

Mind…blown…

"Do you wake up tired?" Nelly asked.

"Every single day," I responded.

"Yeah, I see that you are traveling a lot at night. You are going to a room, and I see a lot of alchemical instruments. Books and weird glass beakers, little fires, magical stuff. You are trying to do something, maybe trying to remember something."

CHAPTER 19

THE DOORS HAVE BEEN KICKED OPEN

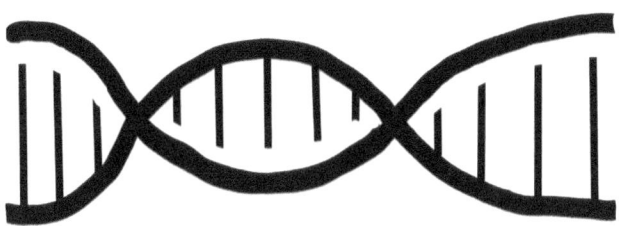

Little things, spiritual things had been happening here and there, but after my session with Nelly, it was like the hinges had been blown off the doors that my subconscious had kept firmly shut for forty plus years.

During random things, the idea of DNA kept popping up. One aspect of this is interesting to me given my background. I worked in a genetics lab in college and eventually entered Grad School to continue that work. That is a story in and of itself but for now, just know that I did complete a Master of Science in Evolution and Genetics.

During all these meditations and sessions with psychics, I kept coming across the idea of DNA and its importance. I just felt like this is the time in the human race's evolution to unlock our dormant DNA. Dormant, or dubbed 'junk DNA' by modern science because we didn't know if it coded for anything. Were ET's helping to activate human DNA? Maybe all the scary stories about abductions by little gray aliens wasn't just about butt probing jokes (see South Park season 1 episode 1) but really it was about unlocking the DNA of specific humans? Many people brave enough to come forward with their abduction or contact stories have admitted that their psychic abilities unlocked afterwards.

I don't know, but I decided to lean into everything. Well, everything but the butt probing and abduction stuff!

During my first meditation after meeting Nelly, I started the practices of calling upon help before my meditations. In one particular session, after asking my guides and Archangel Michael for a safe space to meditate, I requested the six ET guides Nelly spoke of to come to my aid. I asked them to work on my DNA. Random, but I did, and I don't know why that's what I asked.

I cleared my mind, energized my chakras, followed my breathing exercises and waited patiently for something to happen. 'Stuff' doesn't happen every time I meditate, but stuff definitely happened this time!

Out of the dark in my mind's eye a porcelain figure of Mother Mary appeared. You know, the Catholic version commonly seen in stores for sale. Only this version drifted towards me growing bigger and bigger until it was life-sized. Then it slowly morphed in form. It seemed to shift into a porcelain version of Jesus and then back to Mother Mary. The image of Mother Mary slowly faded out and then back into solid form. Finally, the figure lifted its hands to its head and unmasked itself to reveal a female gray ET, like a Zeta gray. It continued to undress itself from the porcelain body suit until it stood fully revealed in front of me. I got the transmission that it didn't mean to scare me since religion is a strong trigger for me. Yeah, the image of Jesus and Mother Mary made me more uncomfortable than the image of a five-feet tall gray alien. Go figure.

Later, many past life regressions would reveal a common theme of my death and execution from the Catholic Church.

The being wanted to work on my DNA. She pulled out a conductor's wand and then six other ET beings appeared. I was laying on a table, the female conductor at my head and three ETs on either side of me. The six ETs lifted their hands above my body and the female began to conduct a biological symphony with her wand.

A bizarre light show formed above my body. A myriad of colors roiled over my body as the six ETs began to move their hands and extra-long fingers. I gathered it was some kind of DNA activation. I also got flashes of twelve stranded DNA instead of two stranded.

Was this manipulation of the tree of life? Were humans originally possessing of twelve stranded DNA with no telomeres capping our DNA and ultimately capping our life span to under 100 years? Is that why deep in history, ancient cultures claimed those that lived before them had lives of hundreds or even thousands of years?

Scientifically, the idea of repairing a person's telomeres would make it possible for a human to live hundreds, maybe thousands of years if the process could be repeated without limit.

Suddenly the light show ended and all the ET's disappeared. Groggily, I opened my eyes and scanned my meditation room. That had been intense. I was so tired I dragged myself to my bed in the next room and fell asleep in the middle of the day.

Weeks later, I began having reoccurring dreams. Each time I would be lying on a table or bed, being blasted by multicolored lights from above. No one else would be around.

The object emitting the lights was in the ceiling and reminded me of the Lite Bright toys we had as kids. But each of the light bulbs shot a laser of light down onto my body. Hundreds of them hitting my whole body. It was like each dream, the lights hit a different side of my body.

Was this interaction with the being a healing, or DNA activation? Or am I just losing my mind?

CHAPTER 20

MERMAIDS ARE REAL, BUT THEY AIN'T NO ARIEL

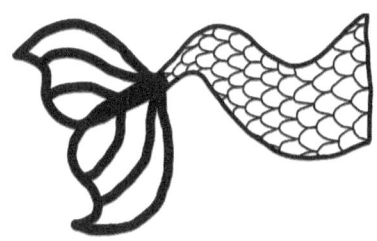

For me, the thing about meditating is learning to let things flow. This is especially true in the early phases of meditation practices.

It is common for things in the day, or something we watched on television the day before, to leak into our meditation. This usually happens in the beginning of a session before we get into the Theta brain state. The hardest thing to do is learn to let 'things' come. If it is fluff from our environment, it will eventually work its way out of our space once we have successfully reached a Theta brain state. It took me a long time to accept the flow and let it do its thing. I usually tried to push it away and then that altered my meditation, and I ended unhappy with nothing much happening during the session. The following experience is a powerful example of why we need to let the flow happen.

My meditation on this particular date started the usual way, asking

Archangel Michael and my spirit team for a safe space to communicate with the universe.

Once I had finished my breathing and chakra exercises, my mind was sufficiently blank. Out of the murky darkness appeared a cuttlefish. The cute little squid species that can change their skin like a cross between an octopus and a chameleon.

The cuttlefish was electric and beautiful, but I thought it was silly, so I pushed it aside. It slowly swam back into my inner vision. Persistent.

I began to push it aside a second time before I remembered the importance of letting things come. Instead, I followed this cute little guy with my astral body. We swam and swam. I felt like we were in the western Atlantic Ocean swimming towards the deeps of the central part of the ocean. Through the blackness I could see the water swirl before me, small bubbles sometimes escaping from my little night light buddy leading the way.

After what seemed like an eternity, the blackness began to lighten up. It was like being birthed into a watery world of magic. I could see the bottom of the ocean and the landscape, but the area above was still inky black. It appeared to be a world under the world.

My little guide began to pull away from me as we approached a literal underwater city. It had the appearance of an underwater medieval village with alien spires reaching up from the ocean floor and a clear dome over its entirety. The structures reminded me of massive sponges, rough exterior and random holes scattered over the exterior. Actually, it kind of reminded me of the exterior of my Spirit Command Center.

There appeared to be one way into the domed city and two Mer-like beings with some types of spears were guarding the entrance. The cuttlefish seemed to signal to the beings and one guard swam out to meet us halfway. The two seemed to converse and then I had the impression that the guard needed to ask permission. The communication was not what I envisioned telepathy would be. It was more that I just knew what the being had to say.

The guard entered the city and left his partner standing watch, looking at me and my little buddy curiously. Well, to be honest I'm sure it was me that was holding his attention.

The other guard returned to his partners side and it was approved. The cuttlefish swirled in front of me and then shot for the entrance. I followed without any hesitations.

Once inside, there was much excitement. More of these Mer-people were gathering in the streets. Well, I don't know if they were streets, but they were traffic lanes running between the building-like structures. Honestly, I felt like the knight prince returning from a successful war campaign, parading down the streets on my way to the palace.

Instead of a palace, I was led to a beautiful park at the center of the dome. The center of the park overflowed with a wide variety of alien plants and seaweed. The male, female, and children Mer-people packed into the park and surrounded me.

Completely unexpected by me, these beings blasted me with what I can only describe as Love Energy. Like their heart chakras spun up vortexes of energy that swirled towards me and engulfed me in pure love, compassion, and appreciation for me. My astral body collapsed to the ocean floor while my physical body back in my home was wracked with sobs. Tears flowed down my cheeks until my nose blubbered. It was a bizarre cross between joy and sadness. Joy at being loved and sadness of reliving what I had lost. But how had I lost this, I've never been here before?

I felt so unworthy of their love.

I asked them to help my path in life. Help me understand what it is I am supposed to be doing.

The beings flooded me with information, feelings, and lessons. They showed me how upset they were with humans trashing Gaia. They told me they had been on Earth for a very, very long time. They were from the Pleiades star system. Their species was like seahorses, the males give birth. They wanted me to spend more time in the ocean, surfing, swimming, paddle boarding, it didn't matter as long as I allowed the ocean to surround me.

Through the many podcasts and videos of experiencers, I have come to an idea related to visitations. I believe that if you are visited by an entity and you feel nothing, then you don't have a direct connection to that type or race of entity. However, if you just physically break down crying or are so happy you are brought to tears, I believe that is recognition on a subconscious level.

It makes sense to me, that your being is recognizing the aura, or genetic DNA, or soul signature of an entity type that you have within yourself. Maybe I had an incarnation as one of these Mer-people and that is why my physical body back in my meditation room was wracked with sobs from the joy of them connecting with me?

Maybe this also holds true for the Sirian contact described in the chapter *The Meditation That Changed Me Forever*.

To lend even more credence to this theory, in two separate Akashic

Readings to examine my star lineage, I was told that I spent two lives in the Sirius star system. Well, the Sirian female life in that meditation makes complete sense for this, but the second life is even more interesting.

There is a group of people in Africa in the nation of Mali that are known as the Dogon Tribe. These people have an uncanny knowledge of outer space and ETs. They make large extravagant masks to imitate the ETs their ancestors were visited by. Specifically, the Nummo, which are described as being related to water and having green skin covered in green hair and being formed like humans from the groin up and serpent-like in the lower body. Historically the Dogon would celebrate the arrival of the white dwarf star, Sirius B every 60 years.

But here is the mind blower. 'Western' civilization learned the Dogon knew about the dwarf Sirius B star in the 1930s. Sirius B is too small to see with the naked eye and most telescopes in the 1930s. Western civilization didn't discover the star officially until 1970.

However, to be fair, astronomers believed there might have been a dwarf star next to Sirius as far back as 1862. Detractors of this story believe that missionaries visiting the Dogon must have told them about Sirius B. But with all the things to discuss with a foreign tribe, why a tiny star theorized to exist? This argument just doesn't hold up in my opinion. I mean, are all missionaries schooled in astronomy, including vague ideas like a theorized star in one of 88 officially recognized star constellations seen from Earth?

There is another angle to this whole idea. Why is it that some people you meet you just instantly can't stand? I believe it is because your soul and their soul have had an incarnation (or multiple) together where you had beef with each other. Or maybe they like you just fine but you can't stand them because their other life they slighted you in some way and your soul memory is holding a grudge.

CHAPTER 21

LIFE KEEPS GETTING IN THE WAY

MARCH 22, 2023

I stared at my computer screen. My wife had recently endured two surgeries and had begun her five months of chemotherapy. Work seemed like a meaningless chore these days. Which was crazy because I had started this business and dragged everyone along until I had made it a success. But the initial creation of success is done and over, it takes constant input to keep something successful.

Ian popped up on the computer screen. "Yo, boss, what's going on?"

"Same old bullshit," I muttered.

"That well, huh? Well, we miss you around here."

I know Ian was trying to be patient with me, but I was the broken cog in the wheel for the employees to keep the business running. It went, quote the client, take the client's purchase order, ship the product, conduct the tech support and initial training to get the client up and running.

I was responsible for the bookkeeping, maintaining stock, and some of the shipping from my warehouse. Knowing my wife's major trials were coming, I had moved most of the shipping to the Midwest where Ian and other employees were stationed.

"I know man, I'm trying to get some bills paid and order more equipment. But I need help man. I'm so overwhelmed trying to keep my home running, kids and dogs fed, and my wife alive. I need you guys to get me a list of what we have in stock right now and what we have in outstanding orders," I grumbled. "Get me that and I can order more stock once the kids are in bed tonight."

"Yeah, we got you. When we hang up, I'll get the guys online and let them know what we need to do."

Honestly, if it wasn't for Ian picking up so much of my slack, our company would be in serious trouble. "Thanks man, I seriously appreciate it."

"No probs. Tell Jennifer I said hi and hope she's getting better," Ian said compassionately.

CHAPTER 22

IT COULD ALWAYS BE WORSE

MARCH 24, 2023

As you can imagine, my chances to meditate got fewer and farther between given all the chaos of our life. However, I still found my chances and took full advantage of them.

One such chance found me drifting through the blackness of space until I returned to the pastoral scene spread out below the hill my Spirit Command Center sits on. This was home. I astrally flew across the landscape in a flash, stopping before the door of my home away from home.

The organic interior was calming. The same long, tall hallway spread out before me with the skinny tables and the wandering robed figures. The door on the right was where I could go to meet my spirit team. But this time the place was different. There was a new door on my left, across from the room filled with spirit guides.

But before I could explore that door, I noticed the sheer massiveness of a door at the far end of the hallway. It seemed almost ominous. But stranger than the door was the figure hovering at the ceiling above that door. It appeared to be the classic Angel from renaissance art works. Male, blonde, beautiful and garbed in leather scale armor over a toga with bare arms and legs, Roman-style sandals. Behind and surrounding this being were clouds and lightning bolts. It wasn't a painting; the being was actually there but the clouds and lightning appeared to be painted on the wall. It reminded me of a Michelangelo painting.

Is he an Archangel? I wondered.

I got the impression he was a 'Watcher'. Whatever that meant.

Suddenly my ethereal body was pulled up and down the hall towards this Watcher. Before reaching the being, I was sucked out one of the coral windows in the ceiling. I became the Watcher, or to be more precise, I think I was drawn into the Watcher's body. Together we began to move through space and time. Our surroundings became an energy tunnel of technicolor. It reminded me of a warp travel in a video game.

We approached what I felt was the end of the tunnel. It ended at pyramids and what I thought was a Stargate. We angled towards the gate and went through it.

Poof!

I found myself back in my own ethereal body. The angel guy was gone. I was on a tiny planet, and I could see a spiral galaxy in the distance. Inspecting my surroundings, I found myself surrounded by what must have been hundreds of pyramid shaped rock piles. They were literally stacked rocks. All about three times as tall as myself.

Turning to take in the landscape, I realized that I was not alone. There was a giant ET watching me. Classic appearance of a Zeta gray but probably ten stories tall. The being was sitting alone, placing another rock on a pyramid stack.

Returning its attention to me, the ET sent a gush of information at me. Again, more like I knew his story than he communicated telepathically.

The poor being was marooned on this red, desolate planet. He was the last of his kind, so there would be no rescue for him. He survived off the energy of the universe and did not eat, but he also could not die. He built pyramid after pyramid to maintain his sanity. They were not toys, but he was trying to create a Stargate to escape this dead planet.

His loneliness caused my physical body back on Earth to burst into tears. Remembering how it felt when the Mer-People blasted me with heart energy, I imagined my green heart chakra spinning faster and faster until I beamed it out of my chest. My green heart energy hit the giant in his chest. I sent love and compassion to him.

The being smiled and thanked me silently.

Then, I shared my memories with him. I gave him images and information about Earth and humans. The lush beauty of Earth's forests and coral reefs, and the art and music humans can create.

I kept using the term 'people' when talking of humans and curiously he kept correcting me with 'beings. Maybe the universal term for sentient entities is 'beings?

After some time had passed, I began to feel a tug on my body. I was being pulled in the direction of the Stargate that I had exited from. I quickly said my goodbyes to the giant and shared more heart energy before I was once again encased in the body of the Watcher, and we were sucked into the Stargate and the technicolor tunnel of energy. Everything flew in reverse until I found myself back in my Spirit Command Center for a split second and then back in my physical body.

I was left exhausted and drained. But I felt good. Felt proud of myself for communicating with that giant ET. I hoped another benevolent species would find him soon and help him escape that tiny, red, dead planet spinning on the outer perimeter of that spiral galaxy.

CHAPTER 23

WHAT?

As my meditations progressed, I sometimes started in one place before flashing into another location during the same meditation. I also began tapping into my Higher Self. When this happened, I could ask questions about the stream of information coming through. The following was the most powerful Higher Self communication rolled into an astral travel that I had experienced to date.

Wisdom comes from ancient places.

I see rock piles. Then, Stone Henge. The Hopi of the southwest. Astronomical knowledge. Sun. Moon. Stars.

Then an image of a rocking chair.

"Is this telling me that I need to contemplate things?" I wonder. "Am I supposed to visit these places," I asked the Ether.

Some yes. Some no.

"Do I visit them astrally or physically?"

Some you will visit in the physical. Some you will only need to visit in the astral. Some are portals to other worlds. Some are communication devices. Shasta has lots of power.

I see huge mounds of dirt. Mistaken for graves. Not sure where these are located. Then I could see pyramids of all shapes, sizes, ages, and construction types. It is common for me to see pyramids in almost every meditation. I don't know why and at this point it is becoming maddening that my Guides won't break down the symbolism behind the pyramids.

Collect Earth energy.

Then I get the impression of a pyramid's energy in my head, it's a blue energy but it doesn't make sense. Now I see the pyramid of Giza and a black stone box. Pretty sure it is the black sarcophagus inside the King's Chamber of the Great Pyramid.

Then any connection that I had with my Higher Self dissolves as I feel my body bio-locate to the Sphinx of Egypt. There are no pyramids in this vision, only the Sphinx and it is new, not weather worn and half rebuilt like it is now.

The head of the Sphinx is proportionate to its body size and bears the resemblance of a jungle cat. As I stand before the great stone beast, its left paw shudders and lifts into the air. Sand cascades down under the paw as it lifts to reveal an opening to a shaft. Once the paw has lifted high enough for a man to walk under, it halts and locks into place. Only dust and sand slowly swirl in my vision.

I feel drawn to the opening and descend the stairs. Bottoming out, the stairs end where a red and black granite square hallway begins. The corridor is perfectly squared off, with what appears to be 90-degree angled corners. The height is enough for me to walk without stooping. In this astral form, it is difficult to tell how far I traveled, but the hallway opens into a larger square room.

I quickly realize this was the same vision I had seen before with the huge Anubis and Horus beings. The room appears the same as before, large square pond with four tall obelisks at the corners and the two god-sized entities in the back of the room. However, two things are different. This time instead of liquid metal, the container in the center is filled with black fluid like liquid obsidian. Also, the image of Horus has been replaced by a huge Pharaoh. Same big body, but the falcon head was replaced with the head of a man with Pharaoh head ornaments. Maybe it was still embodying Horus?

Furthermore, this time the huge Pharaoh moved! The entity stepped to the side to reveal a door in the back wall. Before I could move, I had images flash before me and then I was back in my house.

Uterus - Birth - Life-force - Physical Alter

What in the world did that last message mean? I'm still not sure about the entities and the Sphinx lifting its paw. However, 14 months after this vision, I would visit Egypt and the King's Chamber would indeed be filled with blue energy like my description above.

CHAPTER 24

THE THREE STOOGES WILL LIVE ON FOREVER

MARCH 26, 2023

At this point, my meditations have become much more entertaining than television.

On a rare occasion I got the chance to meditate in the morning. I usually only have time between lunch and around 4pm. Deciding to take advantage of this anomaly, I asked the Universe to speak to me.

After some time, in my mind's eye, I saw two huge figures standing to my left. Turning, thinking it was the Pharaoh and Anubis, I was surprised to see two human-like ETs.

Then I was shown a chair, so I sat. Apparently, it was a seat on a spacecraft. I was on some kind of ship bridge surrounded with panels and the sensation that I was hurtling through space or time, or time and space. There were two little gray, Zeta type ETs standing to my right. So, four ETs total and I was in the captain's chair. I chuckled to myself at the ridiculousness of this encounter.

One of the entities spoke into my mind, Stars are portals to each other.

We traveled into our Earth's sun and into an energy tunnel.

During the trip, the beings showed me a technological device that was amazing. It was like a tablet, but it lays down on the counter and projects up 3D images. They showed me how it could be mentally asked to show anything you wanted to know, and it was flashed up in a hologram. Like a super smooth version of the 'We need you Obi Wan,' message from Princess Leia in *Star Wars*.

I told them I would like to have this device in my life back home. They didn't answer, so I guess that meant it was a no go. Oh well, never hurts to ask.

It was time to disembark the ship, we had arrived. Outside the ship and on the ground, I was presented with a desolate gray world. There were many homes scattered out in front of me. Short for my stature, but it worked for the short gray ETs. Then began the most hilarious cultural exchange that I had ever heard of.

The beings were real jokesters. Called themselves Cosmic Jokers. They love physical comedy and wasted no time rolling out the red carpet. Many of them came quickly waddling out of the nearby homes. They carried interesting chairs and drinking cups. Like an American street party, we lined up chairs facing the street.

They quickly played through some impromptu gags and shticks for me. It was honestly hilarious to see little gray ETs slap each other around and pretend to trip over things.

They love, love expensive Earth human liquor. Looking around, anyone that wasn't part of the comedy show was laughing and swirling their glasses of brown liquor.

They are vegetarians, although I don't remember seeing any plants of any kind.

The Universe is truly vast, and funnier than any of us would believe. Either that, or I have lost my mind but still manage to function normally in the regular world.

CHAPTER 25

TREAD WITH CAUTION

MARCH 27, 2023

Not all that glitters is gold. I learned that lesson during one awkward meditation.

Before beginning, I did my usual prayer to my Guides and Archangel Michael to create a protective space for me to communicate with any beings of love and light.

After some time spent clearing my mind, I found myself standing with my seventeen Guardian Angels surrounding me. They formed a half circle. I looked around to see what was coming next.

Eventually, I noticed a huge entity standing outside the light cast by my group. The being was a shadow with an overly large head. It had to be fifteen feet tall. I could not see any details, just black.

I waited for it to communicate or come into the light so I could get a better look. As my unease began to grow, I said, "If you are love and light, please come into the circle and talk with me."

Nothing. No movement. The being didn't speak or make any motions of any kind.

I asked my Angels to let him in to our circle if he was benevolent.

Nothing.

We all just stood motionless, staring at each other. I was growing more uncomfortable.

At this point I had had enough. I projected myself to my Spirit Command Center and ran to the table with my dragon's crystal and quickly tapped it.

Whoosh!

I was in my dragon's cave. I ran up to Ragnar and wrapped my arms around his neck below his head. A futile exercise considering his neck is as big around as a car.

I ended this session and leapt from my chair. I quickly walked around the house, but the feeling of unease would not relinquish itself. I had to do something.

I tracked down my Palo Santo wood and some white sage. Grabbing a lighter, I smudged my house, room by room. Not leaving the closets untreated, I told every room that "Any beings that are not of love and light must leave now and are not welcome to ever return."

CHAPTER 26

QUANTUM HYPNOSIS HEALING TECHNIQUE

APRIL 2, 2023

QHHT was created by the legendary Dolores Cannon. She developed the technique initially through hypnosis work with her patients. Along the way she discovered that she could connect the patient to their Higher Self, past lives, and channel other beings. She also learned that the body could heal itself if it cleared a past life trauma related to their current life's medical problem.

I stumbled across this modality on a show interviewing Savannah Cosman. She was a Quantum Hypnosis Healing Technique (QHHT) practitioner that kept having clients describe their past lives on Atlantis. Enough clients in fact that she wrote a book about it. I find it is a fascinating process for the practitioner to assemble client's sessions into a chronological and coherent book. After devouring both of Savannah's early books, I delved into the Dolores Cannon books. Those books are more tombs than books. Lots of great stuff about consciousness.

I did some searching for a practitioner in my area and settled on Bev Dovin. She is an amazing woman. My initial call with her lasted for an hour and I literally felt energized for three days after our talk. All these practitioners tend to be booked months out, heck Savannah is booked more than two years out! But the day finally arrived for my session with Bev, and I experienced stuff I couldn't have imagined.

The hypnosis induction process takes you deep into your subconscious. I started on a fluffy white cloud. Then Bev coaxed me off my cloud and down into a past life that was relevant to what I needed to know at that time in this life.

"I want you to tell me the very first thing that you notice down there. Or your very first impressions that you have as you come back down to the surface. Are you, coming off the cloud yet?"

"I just see red." I said slowly and quietly.

"You just see red. Okay. And as you are there, just tell me about the redness that you are seeing," Bev said.

"It is nothingness, it is just red."

"It is just red. And does it seem like light?"

"Hmmm. Just warm and red."

"Warm and red. Any sounds that you notice?"

"No," I said. "The red is changing to white…gray…light gray."

"So, from red, to white, to light gray. Just allow the images to come to you. They will become clearer as you step more fully into them. And are they continuing to change colors or shape?"

"I see shapes and outlines and just gray."

"As you move into these colors and shapes, things will become clearer. Is there anything you are sensing?"

"A pain in my left side," I said slowly.

"Okay," Bev responded. "Right. And you do not need to have any discomfort, you can just be an observer to what is happening. And allow yourself to see and notice what is around you more clearly. Do you get a sense if you have a physical form?"

"It is like I'm in a fog. I see things in the fog. I can't make any of it out," I said.

"Okay. The fog will clear. Just allow yourself to drift and float through the fog until it has cleared. Drifting and floating, drifting and floating. Until you are on the other side of the fog. And can see clearly. And now, you are there."

"It is a red landscape."

"A red landscape. Describe it to me," Bev coaxed.

"Dumb, boring. Shapes, hills, no trees. Shades of red. I feel like I'm bald. I don't have any hair."

"Okay, just glance down to where your feet might be. What do you notice?"

"Hmmm, I'm a grown man…wearing sandals. My side still hurts," I groaned.

"Okay. Allow yourself to glance up your body and describe to me what you are wearing if you are wearing anything."

"It is like a red toga. Goes down below my knees. I feel like I'm holding a golden-colored spear. And like gold something on my head. Clean bald, with a necklace on my head, well not a necklace because it is on my head. Jewelry on my head," I said.

"A gold jewelry on your head. Describe it to me," Bev asked.

"Itssss, small on the crown of my head. As it goes back it gets closer to my ears and then goes down my neck. It might join a necklace. I don't know how it stays on my head…There is no reason for it to stay there unless it is glued on."

Bev chuckled quietly. "Okay are you male or female?"

"I think I am male. There is something wrong with my left side," I answered.

"Okay. Young or old?"

"I am younger."

"Okay. Healthy or unhealthy?"

"I think I'm healthy. But I'm injured on the left side."

"Okay. Alright. Again, you do not have to feel any discomfort. You can just be an observer. And just take a look at the left side and see where the injury is."

"It is right here," I motioned to the left side of my ribcage. "I've been cut by something. Right there," I pointed.

"Okay. And you see a wound?" She asked.

"Yeah. It is cut through my clothing. Maybe that is why my clothes are red."

"Okay. Now just take a look around at your surroundings and see if you notice anyone or anything else around you besides the red landscape."

"I think there is something over there. It's…A hut. It is gold colored like my head thing."

"And you get a sense of what it is made out of?"

"Hmm, it is metal. It is gold metal. Very small."

"Okay. And is this where you live?"

"I don't know. I feel like I want to go there."

"Okay. So, let's drift and float. Leaving this scene. We are going to drift and float to where you are at this hut. Drifting and floating. Drifting and floating. Staying in the same lifetime that we are looking at. But now you are at this hut. Tell me what you notice. What is happening?

"Inside the hut, it is very sparse, but my wife is here and child. My neck hurts too. Something hurt me."

114

"Okay, alright. And again, you do not need to have any physical discomfort. You can be an observer. And tell me what happens next as you are there in the hut."

"She tries to help me," I said. "She has long black hairlike dreadlocks. I am probably not going to make it. I am glad I get to see them one more time," I bit back tears.

"Okay. So, let's drift and float. Drifting and floating to the last day in the lifetime that we are looking at. And again, you can watch as an observer. We are now moving forward to the last day of the lifetime we are watching. And tell me what is happening."

"I think it is the same day. I am laying on like a cot. My wife and daughter are with me saying goodbye." I began to cry. "I am afraid that I can't provide for them." I choked through the words.

"Okay."

"I don't want to leave them alone. My side hurts. I know that is why I am going to die."

"And you worry about what is going to happen to them?" Bev asked.

"Yeah. I don't care about me."

"And what is happening to your body from the injuries?"

"I'm cold. I'm growing cold. My feet are cold. My hands are cold. My life force is leaving with my blood."

"Okay," Bev said calmly. "And now, whatever has happened has already happened. And you are on the other side of it. From that position, you can look back on that lifetime and see it from a different perspective. Every life…has a lesson…and a purpose. And as you look back at that life, what was the lesson for you to learn from it?"

"I was brash. I didn't think anything could hurt me. I didn't think I could hurt myself."

"Okay."

"I was arrogant, and my family paid for it." I sighed heavily, sniffling and taking deep breaths. "It won't be easy for them without me, to provide. I think I got hurt hunting."

"And what was the purpose of that lifetime for you?" Bev asked calmly.

I breathed deeply and exhaled heavily. "Don't hurt the people that depend on you."

"Okay."

"You can't be stupid when someone depends on you. It is not just your life. It is their lives too."

"Right. Okay. You are doing beautifully; you are doing beautifully. Okay, you are on the other side of what has happened. And from that perspective, tell me how the body feels?"

"Ummm, the pain in my side and neck is going away."

"How does it feel now that you are on the other side of that physical realm?" She asked. "What do you notice?"

"I'm looking down at that life. Looking down at that hut, at my body." My teeth chattered. "I...I feel like I have lived many lives like this," I sucked my breath and exhaled slowly. "Where I have died in my teens or twenties. I feel like I fight a lot. I see the spear a lot. Sometimes, it is for other stupid people's things. Sometimes I try to gather food. Sometimes it's animals, sometimes it's man."

I sniffled in a deep breath, exhaling again, still trying to recover from the emotions of that life. "Lots of times it is the spear that kills me."

"In the same spot," Bev asked.

"Yeah, same spot on my side. It is starting to hurt again," I complained.

"Okay, so again, you do not have to have any physical discomfort. You are just an observer. Just release that energy. And as you are floating and looking down at that body, what happens next?"

"They have to go on without me. I can't watch my daughter grow up," I cried. "I feel like it is a lesson that I never learned. I just repeat it life after life."

"I'm not there anymore, I'm on my cloud again."

"Okay," Bev said. "So, let's move away from that scene. And let's leave that person there to continue. You can move forward or backward to find another appropriate place that has information that you need."

When my Higher Self was asked the lesson of this lifetime. "It's important for him to know his mortality. He can't live forever. It's important to take advantage of everyday.

Again. This is another time where a later Akashic reading I received seems to hit this memory right on the bald bedazzled head.

"This may have already come up in visions or memories, but they are showing almost like a desert-like planet," said the Akasha Reader.

"Do you get a color," I asked.

"Reddish, like reddish brownish. It just feels very like dry and almost like you would imagine Mars, but it is not Mars. They are showing almost like pink hues and the thing about this. I'm being shown that as a child in your current life, you had some kind of nightmare about this particular lifetime. Uh, and part of the reason it feels like desolate, isolated. I'm also seeing this reddish skin and kind of a bulbous head."

CHAPTER 27

QHHT PART 2

APRIL 2, 2023

What are you noticing?"

"Lots of colors. Blues…greens. Hmmm, this feels like Earth. Not that last place. I don't know where that was," I said.

"Okay. And again, just allow yourself to settle in. Allow yourself to see. And tell me, what do you notice?" Bev asked.

"Hmmm, farmland. A road. Houses but like, hmmm, rudimentary."

"Okay, and when you say rudimentary, just describe what it looks like."

"Hmmm, the bottom half is stone. They look like probably only one room in them. In the top half is wood and the top is thatch. It feels very medieval. I can see farmers, peasants."

"And let's take a look down at where your feet are. Tell me what you notice."

I sucked in a deep breath and exhaled the information, "Boots on this time. Hmmm, dark brown. Pants. Brown pants, tucked in my boots that come up to my knee. I have a green shirt on. I think I have dark hair. I'm wearing a brown hat. I'm one of these people."

"You are one of the peasants?" Bev prodded for clarification.

"Yeah, peasant or farmer."

"Any ornamentation at all on your clothing?"

"No, it is very plain."

"And are you carrying anything?"

"Hmmm, it is like a hoe with three long pieces instead of a single hoe piece. It must be for weeding."

"Okay," Bev began. "And, um, male or female?

"I think I'm male."

"Young or old?"

"Hmmm, maybe around 30."

"Healthy or unhealthy?"

"Hmmm, everybody here is unhealthy. But I am average."

"Okay, alright. And how do you spend most of your time?"

"Hmmm, the fields. Looks like I do a lot of weeding. For the crops… Gah! There are people coming, they are attacking!"

"Okay."

"They are attacking the people in the fields. Running."

"Okay. And this was sudden" Bev asked.

"Sudden. They just came running out of the trees. These people are animals. They are dressed in black. They are just killing. Everybody. They don't deserve to be on this planet. I'm running down the road. There are houses I'm running through. People are screaming everywhere. I don't have a family. So, I am running on my own. Trying to get away. I'm trying to get to the forest. I think I can make it. They are too busy killing the slow people."

"Wait. It is dark. Full of brambles. I am just crashing through the brambles. I leave the trail so they can't follow me easily. I am just running. Aghhh. No. They caught me." I groaned and curled on the bed in Bev's office. "My right side. My ribs." I groaned and grunted.

"Again, you do not need to have any discomfort. What were you meant to learn from that life?"

"Hmmm. Not to wait too long for the things you want."

"What do you mean?"

"There was a woman that I wanted to marry. Her name was Caroline. I kept telling myself that if I worked harder I would have more to offer her as a husband. But it was never enough in my eye so I never asked her. Then they killed me."

When my Higher Self was asked the lesson of this lifetime. "It's important for him to see how disgusting humans can be. They are fairly better than animals. It is important for him to see that to get away from being animals we need to look inward."

CHAPTER 28

QHHT PART 3

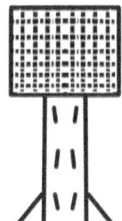

APRIL 2, 2023

You are drifting and floating, floating and drifting to an important time and place."

I exhaled heavily.

Bev continued, "And now, what do you notice? What is happening?"

"Hmm, I'm at a city," I said. "It is not like the world we live in. There are tall buildings, but they are like spires. They are gray. There are people everywhere."

"What do the people look like?"

"Uh, they are not human."

"Just describe them to me," Bev coaxed me along.

"Hmm, they're the size of normal humans…but…their eyes are like humans, but they are solid black, there is no white. Heads are big. It reminds me of old pictures of Pharaohs. They have big heads and kind of like a hat it is almost like cloth, on their head to keep it warm. But there is no hair, and there are men and women, and children. Uh, it's a weird mix of…feels futuristic with the buildings but the clothing is very, everything is handmade. There are no machines, we don't use machines so everything is like, the garments, the threads are so thick you can see them. And the threads, hmm, people don't make their own clothes, there are people that make clothes for us. We don't use machines."

"And how are the clothes made?"

"Hmm, like a long time ago with a big loom and lots of thread. The people move the loom, and the thread comes together to make the clothes."

"Okay."

"Lots of lots of robes, but there is like a cloth with thick threads that kind of come down almost like a tunic that goes over the robes. And the people, eyes are strange since they are solid black. The people…"

"Are the eyes all black?" Bev asked.

"Yeah, solid black like mine. Solid black, no color. And then the head is big. Their arms are normal length, their legs are normal length. I can't see how many fingers they have."

"Did you say they were skinny?"

"Yeah," I answered. "We are all skinny like, like a healthy person that works out."

"Okay, okay, but they have abnormally large heads?"

"Yeah, they are all normal except for those eyes and those heads. And their ears, they have little ears. Little nose. Mouth is normal, I feel they eat food."

"So just take a look at yourself. Look down at your feet and just describe to me what you notice."

"Hmm, my shoes are made of cloth. And I got a green robe on and then my tunic is like everybody else, it is brown. Ha! These people, it is so weird, there are very futuristic buildings but then their clothes are so renaissance-like. And everybody dresses the same, god these people are so boring." Bev chuckled melodically. I laughed, "I mean, they all think alike, that's cool. Everybody gets along. I don't feel like there's music or art."

"It sounds kind of dull," Bev chimed in.

"Yeah, it's really boring, I mean, and the trees don't look like trees. They look like; they look like boxes on top of tree stumps. It is very strange."

"That is strange. And what color are the trees?"

"Hmm, the box part is brown or green and the trunk is normal wood color. And then the houses are cool, they are like, ha, they remind me of a cartoon I saw about this underwater mermaid people, ah the Snorks I think, and they are silver, and they go up" I gestured with my hands. "But they are not normal there are windows in different spots and every floor has a single room and the people. Ha, it's funny. Each person has their own floor and then the ground floor is where they have a place that they eat. But then every floor above it is like, ha, it reminds me of Japanese rooms, very boring like a mat or floor and they don't have beds, they sleep on the ground. Well, they have a blanket or something. And there is a square hole in the floor, and they levitate. I'll be damned! So, they levitate up to the different floors until they get to the floor that they live on. That is why there is no cars or horses or carts because people levitate themselves around."

"Okay, and is the first floor like a communal-"

"Yeah," I interrupted. "The families have floor to themselves, each person in the family and then the first floor is where they live and, and eat together. I don't know where they go to the bathroom, there is no bathroom in here. How can they be so advanced and levitate but be so boring?"

"And do you feel like you are a male or female?"

"Hmm, I think I'm a woman! And I'm so bored!"

"Young or old?"

"Uh, I'm younger, like around 20 or early twenties and I'm so bored. I can't understand how these people can move and get out of bed in the morning. I want to go somewhere, I want to do something, I want to do something different. I don't want to be like these people are. There has got to be something else in this world than levitating up and down floors."

Chuckling, Bev asked, "And how do you spend most of your time?"

"Shit, I just levitate up and down floors." Bev laughed again. "There is nothing to do. There isn't even school…I think we just know. What the hell do we do, we just wander around."

"And is there anything else that is special that you notice as far as abilities? Do the people speak with words or is it more telepathic?"

"Hmm, it is telepathic. We have mouths but we don't use them much. We eat food."

"Then tell me about the food you eat."

"Huh, we conjure it, we don't even grow it. We just think it into existence. God, no wonder I'm so bored. I feel like, I feel like there is nothing outside the city. This culture doesn't have suicide but god if it did, I would have already done it. I feel so trapped and bored, just bored, bored, bored, bored."

"And the type of communication telepathically that you do with each other, what do you tend to communicate about?"

"Hmm." I laughed. "So, we can talk to each other, but we can hide each other's thoughts. So, I can say you look nice in that dress even though I think she looks stupid. However," I boomed loudly. "Families, we put our heads together and we can't hide anything from each other." Very seriously I said, "You only put your head against someone else's head that you trust implicitly because there is too much of a chance that you will find something you don't want to know that they think about you."

"That is interesting," Bev cooed.

"Because there are two groups, there are family groups and deep, deep friends. And when you see them put their heads together, you automatically know those people are family or very, very close. I only do it with my mom. I don't even do it with my dad or my siblings."

"Okay."

"I think I'm afraid of anyone knowing my thoughts. In fact, I do it less with my mom now. When I was younger, I used to do it a lot. But even then, my dad and my siblings, I'm too afraid they are going to find out that I don't belong here. And I, err, I think that I incarnated here by a mistake. Because it is so damn boring."

"Okay. Alright. So, let's leave this scene that we are at right now. And we are going to stay in this same lifetime. And let's just drift and float, drifting and floating to an important day or day where something is happening in this young girl's life on this planet. Drifting and floating, drifting and floating to a day of importance where something is happening. And now you are there."

"Hmm, I'm in trouble. Someone I thought was my friend betrayed me. Everyone knows how much I hate it here now. No one hates it here; I hate it here. Everyone is angry with me."

"Okay, and what is happening?"

"They try and decide what to do with me. They don't even know what to do with me. This has never happened before. How can they be so much higher and be…just so…ugh, I don't like it here. I want to run away but when I look outside the city there is nothing. I just see sand as far as you can see. Which is weird because the city is like, gray and vibrant and has the weird trees but…Ha! Those trees are fake! No wonder I'm so bored! That is why they are square!"

"Ohhhhh," Bev exclaimed.

"They wove these trees," I was practically yelling. "It is a memory they have of what trees were like. Ugh, I'm so disgusted with these people. I just want to leave, and they want me to leave. But they know I will die if I go out there. I know I will die but I kind of don't care anymore. Hmmm."

"So, everything is like a facade?"

"Yeah. It's strange, so much fakeness but it is not fake with those you touch heads. That is the only thing good about this place is, if you touch heads and you can touch heads and live with that person it is wonderful. But…"

"So, tell me a little bit more about the person who betrayed you?" Bev asked.

"Hmm, she was a person my age. I thought we were friends. She touches heads with lots of people. So, I thought I could do it with her but, when I did, my hatred for this place slipped into her mind and it alarmed her so much she ran around telling everyone. There are not that many people that live here. Maybe, hmm, a hundred. These people live, gah," I sounded disgusted again. "They live for sooo long, it takes forever to grow up. But it is even more boring because you are like this big," I moved my hands to imitate the height of a baby. "And you know everything the adults know. And then you just slowly, slowly get bigger." I sighed. "They wove the damn trees. No wonder I hate it here. And I'm standing on the edge of the city. I'm trying to decide if I want to stay or leave. My dad is disgusted with me, he wants me to go."

"And what about the mother?" Bev asked.

"She is torn…she cares for me but, I'm so out of the ordinary for these people that they literally don't know what to do. There is no crime. There is no killing. Ugh, I think I just, I never found my niche with these people. I'm so different. I want to strike out across that desert. I know there has to be something else out there. I mean, where did they come from?"

"Right."

"I think collectively they erased that memory. Even the old people here don't know where they came from. I'm leaving. I'm leaving. I don't care if I die out here." I paused. "I'm just walking. The sand, it is not hot, it's just lots of sand." I chuckled. "I'm a woman, that is why my feet looked so dainty when I looked at them. Um…"

"So, let's just move forward, drifting and floating, and drifting and floating. And staying in this lifetime. We are going to drift and float forward to a day that is important. Drifting and floating, moving forward to another day of importance. Now, you are there. And tell me what you notice."

"Hmm." I took a deep breath in and exhaled. "I walked for a looong time. And now I found a city like the last one I was in, but this one is red instead of gray. It has those same damn trees. I hate those trees. Except here everything is red. So instead of green trees they are shades of red. There is no one here. These dumbasses." Bev laughed again. "When they finally get bored enough, they go make a new city and they just make it a different color and then they erase their memories. Gah, I hate this planet! I'm stuck. There is nowhere to go. I mean, at least red is interesting, I guess. I got bored of gray…Shit there is a green city too. And a blue…ugh. I hate this life."

"And are the people all the same?"

"There are no people at these cities! Only one group of people. Once they finally decide…they don't know boredom, ugh…Once they finally decide they have lived there long enough…there is so much mental power in that big fucking head that they just conjure up," I laughed loudly. "They are so boring! They conjure the exact same city, the exact same buildings, the exact same houses, the exact same freaking fake ass trees, except they pick a shade of color, and they make them all that color. So, there is the blue city, I've been there. There is the green city, I've been there. There is the red city, I've been there." Bev chuckled heartily during my rampage.

"The whole damn place. I've been around this planet going from city to city. I mean at least it is more interesting seeing what colors it has been in the past but that is not that interesting."

"Right," Bev agreed.

"And I just conjure my food. Shit, I'm never going to die. I'm so bored. I don't want to be here anymore. This is just boring."

Bev interrupted my tirade. "Let's just drift and float and let's drift and float to the last day in this lifetime of this girl that we have been watching. Drifting and floating and drifting forward." Bev continued, "To the last day of your lifetime. Again, you can just be an observer. And tell me what is happening? What is making this her last day?"

"I'm in an orange city this time. Just sitting…I guess I'm boring too. I'm sitting in the same house I grew up in. And I'm sitting on one of these cots. I have no idea how old I am. These people live sooo long. And I realized…they don't know suicide. But I've realized not only can I conjure my food, and as a group with lots of brains we can conjure whole cities, I have figured out I can get away. I can make my body disappear and I can go to source. And I do. I blink out and my clothes drop to the ground." I laughed. "It is like Star Wars. When they kill Obi Wan Kenobi. My body just disappears. I finally return to source. Ahhh, thank god. Even this place is just white and boring but now I know I can go do something else."

Bev laughed heartily.

"Ah, god, this feels good," I said. "It's like energy, I can mingle with everybody. It doesn't matter what our thoughts are because everyone knows our thoughts. Doesn't matter what, you can be whatever and do whatever. You're just yellow energy."

"So, as you are on the other side of it now. And you look back at that girl's lifetime what was the lesson or her purpose?"

I began to laugh. "Yeah, don't take what you have for granted. Don't take what you have for granted. Life may seem boring, but nothing is as boring as that was. You have to appreciate every day that sun comes up. Every change of the seasons. The flowers, they grow, and they die. You have to appreciate that. Because in that land there were no plants, there was no nothing. It was so boring. So now I appreciate everything more than I did in that lifetime."

"Okay. And now as she is there with the others. What happens next?"

"Hmm…I just hang out in the energy. I was so alone in that last life that now, I just want to stay here for a while cuz, like I'm just energy and I feel so many other entities and there is so much love, we love each other. No one loved me in my whole life in that last life. So, this is nice. Ah, I feel like many incarnations I have been a loner, so I come back to source."

"It feels good."

"Agh, it feels good. It's like I recharge my batteries before the next incarnation."

"How do you recharge your batteries?" Bev asked.

"Hm, you just absorb everyone else's love and give your love. You don't have a body. You're just light, they are light. They are all part of each other. There is no distinction. It is just like a dimension of light. And you can't tell the difference between yourself and the next person. You are just all light. Like I can't shake hands with anybody. I am them; they are me."

"Right, so you are all one."

"We are all one. It is wonderful. And I come here after my lives because life is so hard in most bodies that I have to recharge and ground myself before the next life. Because that one was boring, boring as shit. I don't want to do that one again. But, ugh, so many lives I've died young, painfully. I need this time in the Source with everyone else. I need this time so that I have enough in me, enough in my soul that when I incarnate, I can get through that life without checking out early."

"Right. And how do you know when you are ready to experience another lifetime?"

"Hmm...I just pop into another life. Just pop into a baby somewhere."

"And how do you choose what your lifetime is going to be like. Is there a process or anyone you talk to, have a discussion as to what you want to learn?"

"I feel like I just know what I want the next life to be. And when I decide what I want it to be, I pop into a baby."

"Okay."

"I just pop into a fetus. And whatever I decided for that life, it is going to happen. Why do I always?" I almost wretched with disgust. "I feel like I...for some reason I have been a soldier many, many, many times. Why do I choose that? I don't like it."

"Is there anyone you can ask while you are there at Source?"

"Ah, good point."

"Maybe they can give you some information about all the different lifetimes you have been choosing and why so many difficult lifetimes."

"It is because that is what I want. But why do I want that? Why do I choose it? They tell me I choose it." I sighed heavily.

"And who are you having a conversation with?" Bev prodded.

"Source…Hmm, nah that's an Angel. For some reason, I feel the strong need to protect the weak. And even though they tell me…I'll probably die young. I still choose that path. Protect the weak. My heart goes out to the weak. I want; I want to protect people. I want people to be happy. I want people to love. So even though, I know it is going to suck, I choose that path anyways. I usually, usually die before I have a family, or I die with little children." My eyes began to swell with tears and my nose began to run from the emotion.

"And why do you choose, you know, to die before you have a family, can they give you that answer?"

"I don't know, they tell me that I'm a martyr. I often choose that. But this time, this time I chose to have a family. This time I chose to be old and have kids and grandkids. I usually die alone somewhere. This time, I want to die surrounded by family. I want to be old. Too many times, I died in the blood and the mud and the guts and the bodies." My voice quivered from the pain of those memories as they flashed through my consciousness. "I don't want that this time. I'm tired of that. So many times."

When my Higher Self was asked the lesson of this lifetime. "Hm, one it was funny. Two we needed to remind him that art is important. Music, art. When he was young, he used to draw. Then he got into photography for a long time. Now he works too much. We hate how much he works.

It was important to show him that to remind him to be better than an animal to be better than Viking scum, really. It is important to look inward to communicate with his spirits and to find art again. It's not good enough just to look at. He has to do something; he has to physically do something."

CHAPTER 29

QHHT - HIGHER SELF; PART 1

APRIL 2, 2023

The fascinating thing about QHHT, is the patient's ability to ask their Higher Self questions about their life once the past life regressions have finished.

"Tell us a little bit about that experience when he was eighteen months old." Bev prodded. "And the car accident where the car was T-boned and his mother ended up paralyzed from the waist down. Um, he was completely spared of any trauma or minimal amount of trau-"

"Yes," Higher Self interrupted. "His Angels came in and with their wings they wrapped around his mother and him so that they stayed together. We could not protect the mother completely because she had her own life path and her own path for her soul and the way it needed to go. So, we wrapped our wings around his father to protect him from going through the windshield because he was needed to raise the boys." Higher Self was referring to my little brother born a few years after the accident.

"And also, because the mother needed him to continue through their soul journey together. It is not the first time they have been together. They have been together as uncle and niece. So, they have been together in past lives. So, they chose to live this life together. But she had things she needed to work through and that is why it happened. It had to happen to her, so we had to protect Matt and his father. So, the Angels came in to allow her to go through what she needs to go through in this life lesson, which we are not sure she has learned it or not. But it was not fair, or, er, fair not fair, fair is not the right word. Hmmmmmmmm. It was not the life path, the soul path of Matt or his father to be injured in that accident. So that is why the Angels came in, we wrapped our wings around them, they were saved, and we protected his mother from having too much damage but the damage that she chose before being incarnated.

I later relayed this story to my mother. We had never in 46 years spoken of the accident. When I told her about the Angels wings, she paused before replying. She said I was teething at the time and fussy. They were driving back from the coast on Thanksgiving morning to get home to family. So, she laid down in the backseat and was holding me during the drive. When the accident woke her, she saw me floating in the air. She said my baby form was hovering and not moving, but debris was flying everywhere. She reached out and grabbed me and then everything moved again and she hit the back of the driver's seat and broke her back. She said the EMT staff at the scene couldn't believe I didn't go out the window or through the windshield. She also went on to explain that I never cried through all of that and for the first two days after the accident, my eyes were blank. There was nothing behind my eyes like my soul had left. She thought I was in shock. But on the third day, my eyes were alive again.

"How about that surfing accident?" Bev was referring to the day in my late twenties when I went out to surf fifteen-foot waves on a surfboard that was too short. It was Thanksgiving Day, the same day of the year as the car accident. There was only a couple of surfers in the water and many onlookers watching from the cliffs north of San Diego. I nearly drowned that day; it was the closest to death that I remember experiencing in this life.

"Hm. Stupid is this one."

Bev chuckled.

"He doesn't know it, but all his angels were lined up next to him sitting on that surfboard ready to go. We saw it coming. We knew it was a time to check out. He has predetermined check out points. We followed him down the wave. We went with him. We followed him underwater. When he saw the bright light, it was us. We asked him if he was ready to check out because this was a predetermined point, and he said no, he was not. So, two Angels grabbed him and pulled him to the surface because he was not going to make it to the surface on his own. Then, he went under again. And we were able to lift him again. It took a couple of times to lift him until the point where he could reach and touch the ground with his feet. But, since it was a predetermined check out point, we decided not to take surfing away from him. We wanted him to continue to surf because he had such joy. If it had been a freak accident or a predetermined check out point, and he went too far down the tunnel and then decided to come back, he would have hated surfing from then on and we did not want that. So, we made sure he did not go down the tunnel. We grabbed him quickly and pulled him up."

Because my car accident with my parents was on Thanksgiving Day, my family no longer traveled on that day, and I was alone in San Diego. I was in my mid-twenties. My friends had all traveled home, so I went to surf by myself. Normally this would not be a big deal, everyone surfs by themselves. However, on this day there was a massive swell rolling into the south facing beaches of San Diego. The surf was triple overhead, which means the face of the waves were about fifteen feet tall. The wind was blowing offshore and creating barrels that were so big an old VW van could have surfed down a barrel wave that day. A barrel wave is the ultimate wave for surfers. It hollows out and the surfer can slide back inside and be surrounded by water. It is also called the 'Green Room' in surf lingo.

Unfortunately, I had left my extra-long surfboard for big waves at home that day. But I didn't want to drive home and back, so I got out in my small everyday board and slinked myself into my skintight wetsuit.

That day was insane. The whitewater from the crashing waves was the size of a single-story house. I paddled forever and was just about to give up when I finally broke through and made it outside the break. My muscles burned like fire and screamed out for relief from the extreme workout.

There was only a couple of guys out there, and of course they had their big wave boards. They probably thought I was insane.

The first wave I tried to drop in on was a beast. The wind pelted me with water, and I pulled back, but not before seeing that the drop into the wave was like looking out the third story window of a building.

I waited until the right time and rolling swell and paddled into a wave that crashed towards the right. I dropped into what would prove to be the largest wave of my life! I went down this mountain of water and the wave seemed to form speed bumps that I dodged until the wave was about to flip over on itself and close out. At that moment I turned left and pointed my board towards the shore to escape the gargantuan water wall about to collapse on my head.

BOOM!!!!

The shear air pressure from that much water crashing behind me blew me off the front of the surfboard. I was tossed like a dirty dog toy into the washing machine of highly aerated water. I wasn't under for long and made it back to the surface and began the long paddle back out.

I was exhausted. All the muscles in my upper body burned and screamed for oxygen. Just as I was about to give up, I made it back out past the break. This time I rested for a bit before dropping into a left sided wave. This was more difficult for me to surf because of the way I stand on my surfboard. Like being right or left-handed, every surfer has a strong side and weak side. This wave was just as big as the last but this time I failed to dodge one of the speed bumps in the wave. My surfboard launched me into the air. My feet went out in front of me, and I landed on my back. I was moving so fast it was like hitting dirt. The momentum carried so much speed that I skipped across the water three times like a rock flung at a pond by a child.

After the third skip, I was mid-air when I looked up at the immense wall of water coming down at me. The wave crashed down upon me with the volume of dozens of Olympic sized swimming pools. Collapsing my body into a ball, I wrapped my arms around my knees, but the power of the water ripped my arms out to my sides. Thrashed up, down, side to side until it lessened enough for me to reach for my safety net, the surf leash.

Luckily my surfboard leash was still attached to my ankle. Grabbing the leash, I tried to pull myself to my buoyant surfboard which should have been at the surface. Unfortunately, when I grabbed my board, it was still underwater.

A chill shot down my spine and out my arms. This meant my board had been snapped and the piece still attached to me was too small to float to the surface under the power of the water and my depth.

At this moment I quietly told myself not to panic or I would die. Then my life flashed before me in a series of memories. Years before this I had experienced the same in a near car accident on the freeway. Only this day, the stream of memories was much longer than the time I nearly crashed my truck on the freeway. I wonder if that was because I was closer to death on this day than that near car accident?

I thrashed and pumped my arms and legs with everything I had to get to the surface. Then the brightest whitest light entered my mind's eye. It was like a spotlight shining through my tightly shut eyeballs.

This is it, I am going to see the wizard, as lifeguards would say.

Miraculously, I ripped through the water's surface. This must have been when the Angels pulled me up and saved my life.

I was far from out of trouble. There was just enough time for me to suck in a fraction of a breath before I was pummeled by the next wave. I was thrashed about with almost as much force as the first wave and I barely made it back to the surface before I would have blacked out. My tiny piece of surfboard was more of a hinderance until I made it to the beach and crawled out of the churning waves on my hands and knees.

I dragged myself up the beach and kissed the sand in front of me. Then collapsed on my back, gasping for breath and trying to slow my racing heart. It was the most exhausted I have ever been in my life, before or since. Well, at least in this particular incarnation.

CHAPTER 30

QHHT - HIGHER SELF; PART 2

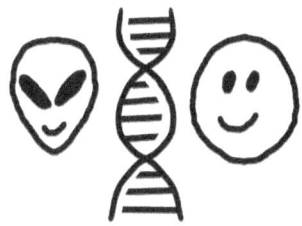

APRIL 2, 2023

"One of Matt's questions was if he has ever been visited by Extraterrestrials?" Bev asked.

"Hm, they come to him sometimes at night, but they leave his body alone. They mentally work on his DNA."

"Okay, okay," Bev replied. "Is there a coincidence with Matt choosing, you know biology major and genetics?"

Quickly and without pause. "He was a Sirian in a former life. He loves science they love science. They were part of the early genetic manipulations on this planet. That is why he went to genetics."

"Okay. Was Matt part of that?"

"Yes. He had to leave. He was a woman. He had to leave with all the Sirians, and it hurt him very bad to leave all his children, the humans. He felt like he abandoned them, but it was just one more type of abandonment that he had to go through. For the times he was a soldier with children, or he was a hunter and died and left his children. The Sirian felt the same experience as she hurtled through space back to where they lived. She felt devastated for leaving the humans. This body is broken because he is constantly leaving the ones he loves, or she sometimes we are she's. And it hurts. Hurts the heart."

"Is that, um, connecting to his heart, to his arrhythmia and stomach?"

"Yeah, his heart affects the stomach pain next to it. But I think we can work on that now that he is learning all these things. I think we can. The heart is good, he fixed that with the doctors, but we think we can fix the stomach or at least lessen the acid pain he feels. The acid reflux we can push that down."

"Okay, and how are you going to do that?"

"We will change the chemical composition of his stomach, so it does not create as much acid."

(See Chapter 6 for the discussion of the past life regression and my later Akashic Reading that relates to my past life as a female Sirian. This is three different sources relaying the same information.)

"Matt needs to trust himself more," Higher Self said. "Things come to him. He doesn't know where it comes from. Sometimes it is something he saw or read and comes to him when he needs it. He just needs to let go, he's so stubborn. He just needs to let go. Things pop in his head; it's us telling him. He just needs to say, 'Oh hey, that pyramid is a great fucking idea. Let's build it'. Oh, well you can't build it because you work too much, you dumbass."

Bev laughed again.

"You gotta hire more employees so they can do the work for you. It will be the same as doing art, it will be doing something with your hands." The Higher Self's speech sped up. "It will be creating power. Then! When you sit in that pyramid and meditate with what we have told you, with the copper wiring filled with quartz and run water inside the wiring inside that pyramid with the limestone siding. Then we will blast the shit out of your third eye."

"So, tell us, is there a specific reason that he is 'so obsessed with pyramids?'"

"It's because he is supposed to build that pyramid. Once he sees the power of that pyramid to help people unlock, like he is trying to unlock himself. He will realize he can help people that way. He can build them for other people. And the fascinating thing is, it doesn't matter where it is on the planet. The planet is the energy. And the pyramid shape captures the energy and funnels it through the pyramid. Helping the person open their third eye and unlock their consciousness so they can communicate with their guides and themselves, and anyone else from anywhere. They could be from other planets that can come in and communicate with them. The idea of the copper on the inside and quartz and running water through it, that is because this vessel goes overboard with everything. Ask him how messed up his body is from all the stuff he's done. So technically, he doesn't need to go that far, but if he REALLY wants to, he can go that far and, shoot, he can astral travel to the sun and inside and teleport to other universes if he really wanted to."

"The pyramid we downloaded to him, which he thinks is his own brilliant idea."

Bev chuckled again.

"Is super powerful. It's obviously not as powerful as what was built in Giza. That, we, we did a number on that, that was awesome until forces like those stupid Viking's came in- They weren't Viking's of course, but it was the same thing. Men of tiny value and no better than animals ripped the guts out of the pyramids, pulled the wires out and ripped the siding off and destroyed the power that was coming through that and feeding Earth. But any pyramid by its very shape and set on the ground, as long as there are sides- Haha, those people on Etsy are idiots. Just the copper pyramid that you walk through with no siding doesn't do anything. The energy just goes straight up and out the top. It has to have sides. The sides are the sides are the sides are the sides. They keep Earth energy inside" My Higher Self said emphatically. "And that creates a vortex inside and that energy can power the Higher Self and the chakras above our body chakras and can help us unlock and open our third eye. He is beginning to open his third eye now. But if he really wants to blast himself, he can do that."

"Okay, maybe after listening to this he will be motivated to build it," Bev said.

"Okay. Matt would like to know if he is on the right path, if he is going to accomplish his mission for this life?"

"He needs to know his pyramids, he needs to know he needs to make money but not focus on money. His current view of money is good, he just says, 'I have enough money, and it comes when it comes'. That is a good way to put it. But at this time, we cannot tell him what his mission is, just that to know his angels are with him and they will guide him to be sure he stays on this mission. Because his guides love him, but they don't want to come back and do this again. Just like no one wants to do the same thing over and over and over again. Which is funny that he wanted to be a soldier over, and over, and over, and over, and over again. And then we had to give him all this pain because he just wasn't remembering. He could have remembered easily if he hadn't of blocked it all out before he was a teenager. But he blocked it all out, so we had to do this."

"So, tell us a little bit about that because Matt says he has very little recollection of his life before the age of 13 or 14."

"That is because his current soul isn't the original soul. It was the original soul, but it was not the original soul. He chose that but then he was taken out of it when he was in that car accident. And a different soul was placed in that body. When he was ready to return to the body, he switched places with the soul and when he switched places with the soul that is when all his past life echoes came about. Whether it was his heart condition or his back injury, or his back pain. Those came about because his life echoes were trying to remind him of his previous lifetimes. That is also why he hates the military, he hates all things military, he hates the police, he hates anyone with a gun. He hates anyone with a weapon because he's had to live those painful lives trying to protect the weak. He didn't always protect the weak. Sometimes he was put in a life, and he was put on the wrong side of the war, he fought on the wrong side. That happens. Everybody does the wrong thing sometimes. That is part of your contract. If you don't go through your contract and find yourself on all sides of the coin. And when I say coin, I mean like a dodecahedron die like they use in their silly board games. You have to see the many facets of it. And that is why your soul fractures over and over and over again to the many different lives. So, you can be a good guy, a bad guy. This particular incarnate insists on being the good guy over and over and over again. Even if it brings him nothing but physical and emotional pain. Leaving him dead on a battlefield. He chooses it and that is what he has chosen. And he wasn't remembering so when we put him back, we had to start injuring him to remember things."

"He didn't have to hurt himself. He had plenty of friends that did the same amount of stuff he did, whether it was surfing or skateboarding or snowboarding or playing hockey. All those friends did the same thing and none of them hurt as much as he did. We had to hurt him to remind him. Whether it was breaking his wrist, which he had done in a previous life. Or the stomach pain because he has been stabbed and shot and killed and everything else. We had to remember and remind him and if he had done this earlier in life, he would have less aches and pains. But now that we are here, we can relieve many of these aches and pains because he will remember this. He won't even have to listen to the recording. He's conscious now, he's just standing off to the side listening to this whole thing. So, you didn't need to cheat with the recorder to begin with. But he's stubborn and he wants to make sure he doesn't miss out on anything which is why he's always hurting himself. But the point is, we can relieve many of these pains now and he needs to remember these lives and understand that when things pop in his head, it's supposed to be there. It is not him having a random idea from something he saw on TV. We are putting it in his head."

"So, tell us a little more about that palace that he goes to?" Bev asked, referring to my Spiritual Command Center where my guides seem to reside.

"Hm, that is his spiritual center. It is where his guides stay. It is where his connection with his other Echoes is. And by Echoes, I mean, pieces of his own soul. So, when he goes into the room with the tree and sees the tree and he sees all the little children of all types of shapes and sexes, those are his Echoes of his same Oversoul that are living their own lives on their own planet. But they all have a connection to the Root; it is just most people never get to see that. He is actually quite blessed for getting to see that. Very few people see their Soul Echoes."

"And Matt says that he heard something walk around his tent-"

"Ha!" Higher Self interrupted.

"In Northern California."

"He knew what it was. He knew what it was. He knew what it was. It was a Bigfoot. A Bigfoot saw his light in the forest. Could sense his Angels with him and the Bigfoot came in to take a look."

"Ahhhh," Bev said. "That's nice."

(This question was also confirmed later in a session with the powerful Remote Viewer Kathy Marjorie.)

"He asks, what is the best way to unlock his psychic abilities?" Bev asked.

"Hmmm. He may never have more than he has now. But what he has now may get stronger. But it is to be determined if we are going to give him more abilities than he currently has."

"Because it seems like he has actually quite a bit."

"Hmmm. He thinks it would be cool to see fairies and dragons. But if we let him see, he will see ghosts and that will eventually freak him out."

"Okay, perfect. But if he understands that there is nothing to fear from it…"

"We could unlock that for him if he understands."

"Okay, on Monday of this week, during his meditation he saw a figure in shadow come to the edge of his spirit space."

"Mhmm."

Bev continued, "And he asked the Angels to let him in if he was of Love and Light, but this figure stayed outside of the space. Can you-"

"The figure was unsure of what to make of him. The figure is not of this world or dimension. The figure noticed him and came in to get a closer look. And as he came in to get a closer look, it is a he, he was unsure of what Matt was and his Angels were rather imposing. So, when Matt asked him to come forward, he was scared. It was not Matt that was scared. He was scared to come forward. So, the link between the two beings was not accomplished. So, it did scare Matt quite a bit. He is silly. His house doesn't need to be cleared. He clears it every night before he goes to bed. Even if he forgets to put the egg in place, his subconscious places the egg before he leaves his body to visit the Federation in the spaceship above the planet. But if the sage makes him feel good, he can do it."

Bev laughed.

"But it is important for him to always clear the crystals before he brings them into the house because crystals have memories, and not all memories are good. So, if he clears the crystals before he brings it into his house, he can repurpose the crystals for his own needs and purposes."

CHAPTER 31

MANTIS BEING

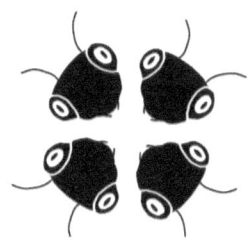

It was early spring. I was struggling to get the kids out the door and off to school. Always a battle. Once in the car, we got some music going so the kids were less likely to fight. My brain wandered from the traffic to what I needed to do for work to the fact that I needed gas. All the while I had a little bit of anxiety and the odd feeling that someone wanted to give me a message. I needed to meditate if I were to receive that message.

Once I got home, I went to my meditation chair and got settled. Morning meditations were unusual for me and this experience would prove to be just as unusual as the timing.

I went through the protocol I had adopted for myself. Focus on grounding. Activate each chakra. Focus on breathing. Blank the mind and wait to see what happens.

After some time, my teeth began to chatter. Much later I would realize this happens to me when a Mantis or Mantid ET being is trying to make contact. Weirdly, my teeth don't chatter like I'm cold, but instead it is almost like speech. My teeth more click than chatter.

In my mind's eye, the Mantid being presented itself to me. About seven feet tall, green in color like our praying mantis here in North America. It was also wearing gold-colored robes. I have a Mantid in my spirit team but this being was different.

I got the word "Antares". At the time I didn't realize it was a star system. Antares is a very bright star in the central part of the Scorpio constellation. This star is the 15th brightest star in the night sky here on Earth. Interestingly enough, my daughter is a Scorpio.

I also received some sort of coded message. I saw a series of shapes that started as an upside-down triangle, then a downward facing crescent, then a UFO shape, followed by a 3D pyramid and finally something like an infinity symbol.

Next, I saw the image of a wolf. Blue and white sphere or planet. A snake or reptile. Then nausea came over me and I began to drift out of my meditation.

But before it was finished, I got the strangest feeling that I needed to visit Giza for some unknown reason.

A few days later, while driving to get the kids from school, I got slammed with an old memory. I remembered that about twenty-five years earlier I had some missing time episodes. Living in San Diego, I would drive north to central California to visit my parents for the weekend.

Once I got through Los Angeles and the mountains and into the valley of California, stuff got weird. During my early to late twenties, I remember many, many times when I would blank out and then come to two hours later and pulling into my parents' driveway. Or sometimes I would regain cognizance and I'd be taking the exit off the freeway to my parents' town.

I am pretty sure this is the definition of missing time in the world of UFOlogy. I'll have to revisit this at some point.

CHAPTER 32

WHAT IS THE DEAL WITH EGYPT?

APRIL 11, 2023

I was taken to the Sphinx again in a meditation. My blue ET Ascended Master guide riding my coattails. This time, the left paw of the Sphinx was already hovering in the air. The entrance to the underground beckoned us.

We traveled down the stairs and the red granite hallway to the room where Anubis and the Pharaoh awaited. Standing guard in the back of the room as usual, the two supernatural beings are more than a little intimidating. This time the Pharaoh was already standing away from the door behind him and looking at that door. Before we could move, the Pharaoh shrunk down from his giant size to a human size that could navigate the doorway.

My blue buddy and I followed the Pharaoh through the doorway and into another hallway, but this time it was more like a rough tunnel than an engineered hallway. The ceiling and walls seemed scraped or chiseled.

Much more natural in substance than the perfectly rectangular red granite hallway that led from the Sphinx paw to the first room.

We walked until we entered a room with four doors. In the center of the room was a very large crystal pyramid. Somehow, I knew it was a repository of knowledge. But I was warned not to touch it because it would harm me.

Next, we went through the center doorway on the far side of the room. To this day, I still wonder where the two side doors go.

Through the center door, we were met by a Mantid being. It acknowledged us. I wondered if it would have been less friendly if we were not being led by the Pharaoh?

The Mantid led us further down the tunnel. Eventually, after an unknown distance and amount of time, we came out into a huge cavern. A very tall and unfathomably old non-human being sat on a massive throne. He was surrounded by futuristic looking vehicles and artifacts. The discrepancy between the oldness yet the futuristic look of everything was jarring to me. There was not a fleck of dust on anything.

As I had learned around other benevolent or benign beings, I sent my love and heart energy to the massive being. I aimed the energy from my chest to his chest. The being grinned and seemed to enjoy it very much.

I asked if he could give me a gift to help humanity.

The being manifested a black-colored pyramid in his hand. The elder leaned forward and presented me with the strange object.

Telepathically, I got the message "Place it on illness".

I asked how to make it, for a download. I was shown my meditation pyramid download but in miniature form. Something about the pyramid corrects the bodies resonance.

Does this have to do with the harmonics of Earth known as the Schumann Resonance?

Is human health related to realigning our resonance with that of Mother Gaia?

CHAPTER 33

MANUAL LABOR FOR YOUR SPIRIT, YOUNG GRASSHOPPER

Many meditations, I just sit quietly and see blackness. Nothing happens. But this day, something unique took place.

The black world in my mind slowly shifted to a gray fog. This was unusual. After some time, the foggy environment shifted to a sunny day. The area looked like a farm with an old white farmhouse at the top of the hill. I was presented with a wizened old person. They appeared so old, and stoop shouldered that given their nonbinary clothing, I could not make out their sex.

I walked up to them to introduce myself. The old person spoke, revealing his sex. "My name is Imhotep." Somehow, I got the distinct feeling that they were an Ascended Master.

"Do you know why I'm here?" I asked.

He grinned and pointed at a field. Gazing at the field, I recognized the tops of carrot plants popping out of the ground. The carrots were arranged in neat rows of furrowed earth. Just like the home gardens I had with my kids, only this was in a much larger size.

Imhotep slowly walked over to the edge of the field where a table and a chair waited for him. The chair was occupied by a woman with curly dark hair, but she got up and offered the old man her chair. Once he was settled, she turned and walked up the hill towards the farmhouse without a word.

Interestingly, there were a few other people in the field near the table with Imhotep. They were on hands and knees harvesting the small carrots.

Imhotep motioned for me to join them. I may not have been keen on the idea of digging up carrots, but you don't exactly deny an Ascended Master. So, I grabbed a bucket from his table and joined the others. Digging up carrots with my hands.

"Gaia can provide all," the old man stated. "It is important to connect to Gaia on a primitive level."

When I come across entities that are willing to name themselves, that is when the research begins. With such an odd sounding name, I felt like it was maybe Sumerian, and I might be able to find reference to "Imhotep".

I was wrong about Sumerian but not disappointed. Imhotep was the Chancellor to Pharaoh Djoser and High Priest of the Sun God Ra, and possibly the architect for the Djoser, or Stepped Pyramid. Not a lot is written about Imhotep from that era. But with time, the Egyptian people eventually deified the man as the God of Medicine and Healing and eventually equated him to Thoth. Thoth was the god of architecture, mathematics, and medicine, and patron of scribes.

The connections between my astral travel type meditations and the fact that I have a Spirit Guide that calls himself Pharaoh Cheops and now Imhotep just keep adding up.

I don't believe these were the same entity. It is possible that Imhotep brought knowledge to the Egyptian people early on. Then later, Thoth also brought knowledge along with the major Egyptian deities that we know more about because they are more recent than Imhotep.

Purely conjecture on my part.

But again, with the ancient Egypt connection in these meditations. Maybe I had a past life in Egypt? Well, I did see that Sirian life in Egypt, but maybe I also had human incarnations too?

CHAPTER 34

CONTACT?

That very evening, I took the dogs out to pee one more time before bed. It was about 9:30pm. My daughter had come out with us. We were looking up at the stars when she pointed out how many planes were out at that time. There actually was a lot. But not surprising as we live in a flight path about forty miles south of an international airport on the east coast.

While we were watching, I saw a far-off light drift out from the Big Dipper constellation. Having spent twenty years out in the field before sunrise conducting bird surveys, I was quite familiar with satellites in the night sky. This object reminded me of that. It moved from west to east/southeast for some distance. Then it disappeared and I thought that was odd given the clear night.

It suddenly reappeared where I expected it to be but this time it had changed its direction to northwest. Almost the complete opposite direction it had come!

It had changed direction by about 165 degrees. The object suddenly got really, amazingly bright white and then disappeared one final time.

Was that a manifestation of my consciousness? My daughter didn't see it, so maybe.

Was it a non-human craft popping in and out of our dimension? Seems like for ETs to travel space they would need the ability to jump dimensions to cover the vast distances of space.

A few months later, I was back out with the dogs before bed. It had become my ritual to watch the stars while the dogs took care of business. I had not seen anything as wild as that last UFO, literal unidentified flying object, that shot out of the Big Dipper. But this night would show me something different but still odd.

I saw a bright orange flash in the sky. Just flashed and gone. It definitely got my attention and single-minded focus. Then to the right of that flash, like it was cloaked and traveling through the sky, the same orange flash reappeared. The trajectory was correct. It was like it was blinking in and out of existence on a straight path. Or its shielding was working, failing, working, failing, working.

I followed the trajectory and waited a couple of minutes but did not see it again.

Was this a ship in distress? Or maybe it was a non-human ship blinking in and out of our dimension? Shifting between this dimension that we see and another dimension they can perceive but we cannot?

I had watched a show about a guy that could point into the night sky and ask UFOs to appear. Right on camera, white lights would appear where he pointed and then shoot off at inhuman speeds.

So, I took the dogs out that night after seeing the show and tried it. I calmed by brain and asked to see them and held my hand up towards the north.

Within seconds, a super-fast flash from right to left and down towards the horizon appeared and disappeared. Then it reappeared and shot up away from the horizon and to the right. Again, it reappeared a third time and shot back almost 180 degrees from where it had first appeared and tracked.

That is the only time it ever worked. I've tried many times since then to no avail.

So, was my consciousness prompting this behavior?

If another person was with me, would they have seen it?

Did I communicate with a non-human intelligence that granted my wish? I don't know for sure. But I feel very strongly that this was not a black ops secret military ship piloted by humans.

CHAPTER 35

THE DRAGON REALM

My meditations all have the same wind up, but how I decide to meditate is often different. Sometimes I feel the need because I sense an entity or spirit has a message. Sometimes I just need to chill out from the stress of life. Sometimes I don't set any intention because I want to see what pops up. Lastly, I sometimes set a specific intention before beginning.

This was an intention day. I set up my safe spiritual space for the meditation, asked Archangel Michael, my guardian angels, my ascended masters, and my spirit team to create a safe space for me to communicate with any benevolent beings. Specifically, I requested to communicate with my Higher Self or future self. I desperately wanted to contact a higher density future version of myself that I could trust to share some wisdom with me.

When the blackness of my mind's eye cleared, the first place I found myself was my Spirit Command Center. At this point it seems I no longer have to go the long route to arrive. Now, I just pop up in front of the building or just inside the door.

The first thing I felt pulled to was my Soul Tree room, first door on the left. I entered the room and looked at my tree surrounded by my children-shaped Soul Echoes. One of these days I'm going to figure out how to communicate with those echoes of myself. I'm especially interested in the obvious ET versions of myself.

Next, I was drawn up to the Watcher Angel entity in the ceiling. As before, I was drawn into his body and we left the building and shot into the Void. Unclear of where we could be going, I was surprised to suddenly see my dragon, Ragnar, flying around us through the void. Before I knew it, I felt my Astral Body pulled out of the Watcher and onto Ragnar's back. Just like all kids dream, I was riding on the back of a massive dragon!

We continued through the Void, towards a yellow light that grew into a yellow sun. Much more yellow than Earth's sun. Then we suddenly popped into another reality, a fantastical world. Beautiful. Lush. Green. Blue sky.

This world reminded me of a Ghibli movie. Technicolor, with huge chunks of earth floating through the air. I can't see any ground below us. It just seems that all these floating islands were the totality of this world. They were covered in grass and forests. Rivers meandered across their faces until falling off the edge and disappearing into the mists below.

And Dragons!!!

Hundreds, no thousands of dragons! Every color and size, every shape a human could imagine. Fantastical dragons, wingless serpent dragons, wyverns, tiny dragons.

Just as I wondered where we were, the word "Anaphase" popped into my head. Anaphase, the land of Dragons. Or at least this particular Dragon Realm was Anaphase.

All the dragons were flying alongside us. I could not help but think of the How to Tame Your Dragon movies. It was so magical I hoped it would never end. Maybe the realness of this realm is why that movie resonated with so many people? Maybe our human race has a species memory of a dragon realm?

Eventually, I realized why all the dragons were flying in the same direction. We were all headed to a large island with a colossal opening in the forest. It was surrounded by trees on three sides and butted up against a big, barren stone wall forming a natural amphitheater. All the dragons landed creating a semi-circle around the stone cliff and bowing to their waiting king. The leader of these dragons was old and wizened, white and gray. I got the sense it was male, and it reminded me of a Chinese dragon with bushy eyebrows and whiskers from its snout, but with wings.

While I sense the other dragons, including Ragnar, couldn't speak vocally, this elder could and spoke clearly. "Ragnar speaks very highly of you," the old dragon's voice rumbled, reverberating off the stone wall behind him.

"I'm pretty low on the totem, so I don't know how high his praise can actually be," I joked.

The old dragon boomed a hearty laugh. It cascaded across the watching dragons, and they jostled each other, cooed and cawed, grumbled and growled, rustled their wings and shook their heads. As the ground rumbled under my feet, I thought to myself this scene would make a great kids movie.

"Yes, you and Ragnar were made for each other. Now then, this is an important time for humans and your type has much potential."

I was in awe at this old dragon and his ability to speak. We continued to discuss things for some time but unfortunately, I can no longer remember the topics. They slipped from my consciousness before I could record them in my journal. It is very frustrating when that happens, most commonly in my dreams.

Finally, he boomed, "*Enough!*"

Dragons scattered everywhere. Ragnar quickly moved forward and put me on his back and launched us into the air. That was it, I guess. When the King says he's done, he's done.

CHAPTER 36

CETACEANS ARE JUST AS MAGICAL AS DRAGONS

MAY 14, 2023

Sometimes life gets in the way. Life had gotten busy and it had been quite some time since my last meditation that took me to Anaphase. I felt the strong pull to get back into a regular meditative practice.

On this day, I felt myself go really deep into a Theta brain state.

Then I was floating deep in space. I floated for quite a while, unsure of what I was supposed to see or learn in this space.

Something moved behind me and I spun to find a space whale! It must have been Cetacean Consciousness because as I watched, it changed form. Sometimes it was a huge blue whale, then morph down into a smaller California gray whale, or grow into a larger humpback whale.

It told me that my big aura and my Guardian Angels are so bright that I stood out. It told me that animals come to check me out because they can see my aura and Angels. At the time, I did not know what this entity meant, but I would soon have it validated by a talented psychic during a session of exploration.

It was like the whale projected images into my head. I saw a Bigfoot, the times I surfed alongside dolphins in real life, and the gray whale that came up to our small boat when my dad and I were ocean fishing off California. The flash of information into my brain was so fast I almost didn't catch it all. It reminded me of seeing my life flash before me when I almost drowned in my surfing accident so many years ago.

The encounter enforced the feeling I have that my Guardian Angels and spirit team have me covered and supported in this incarnation.

CHAPTER 37

BIGFOOT?

We have to go back two decades to discuss these encounters.

I was in my late twenties when I was in graduate school. I worked my way through college and should have walked away with a PhD for how long it took me to get an Associate's, Bachelors, and Master's degree. But, for as difficult as it was living paycheck to paycheck, those years were a blast. I was being paid to conduct bird counts, working on cutting edge genetics studies for my Master's thesis, dating my future wife, and surfing as many days a week as I could pull off. It was a magical time looking back on it.

My thesis was researching a species of montane woodpecker in California. To do this, I spent two summers camping all the California mountain ranges above 4,000 feet. There were a few excursions that my thesis advisor traveled with me, but most of it was solo. It was a grand adventure. In California, once you get to higher elevation, you can explore the logging roads for a lifetime. I just car camped up and down the state. It was simple to pull off the dirt road into a flat area, setup my tent and make my peanut butter and honey sandwich for dinner and hit the sack at sunset. It was very minimalistic. No ice chest, no campfires, no cooking. Once a week I would leave the backwoods to find a cheap hotel to shower and do laundry.

I grew up in California, fishing, hiking, snowboarding, and exploring the Sierra Nevada with my dad and brother. Thus, I felt at very comfortable in the mountains of my home state. Up above the rattlesnakes, ticks, and poison oak are the best parts of the snow and surf state.

With that being said, I can't deny there were places that gave me strange or uneasy feelings. Those feelings could be amplified if I hadn't passed another truck or seen another person for a few days. Many times, I felt like I was being watched. Was it the ghost of an old miner from the gold rush era? A mountain lion or bear? Or something more cryptic?

When these feelings sent chills down my neck, I told myself it was a cougar, and I raised my guard and left the area. There were times my hair would raise on my neck and arms. The flight part of fight or flight would kick in so strong that I would back out of the area and drive a mile before stopping again to resume my search for the elusive woodpeckers.

A few specific events from that time have always stuck with me. And if the boom of searching for Bigfoot television shows had happened before my bird research, I would have realized that I was finding Bigfoot sign all over the mountains of Northern California.

While in the Lassen Mountain area, I stumbled upon an opening in the forest that left me scratching my head. A large area had been turned into a meadow when the pine trees died. Only this wasn't normal death. These trees were upside down in the ground. The root balls of the trees were where the treetops should be. Examining the trees, I found that the airborne root balls were about fifteen to twenty feet in the air. At the time, I couldn't figure out why loggers would bring heavy equipment this far out just to rip trees from the ground and then bury them upside down. As anyone that watches a lot of Bigfoot shows knows, this was a territory sign. Likely a group of Bigfoot did this to show others that the area was occupied or some such display.

While near the Oregon border, I was in dense forest. It was not the more open, dry pine forests of the mountains on the east side of the state. This area in the North Coast Range is dense, with lots of berries, bears, deer, and elk. While staying here, I just had an odd feeling every day, all day. I was on alert the entire time, from sunrise until I passed out from fatigue after sunset.

One evening, I couldn't find any place to pull my truck over and setup my tent. So, I just parked in the narrow road and setup my tent in front of my truck on the logging road. I had taken to blasting the radio in my truck in areas that creeped me out. I guess I hoped the noise would keep the bears and cougars away. I never thought it might bring in something curious.

With my meager, sad little dinner finished, I turned off my truck ignition. Immediately throwing the surroundings into the same deathly silence I was trying to mask with the music. Within seconds, I heard a god-awful scream of some sort. It chilled my heart. I did a quick scan around me and jumped into my single cab pickup. Quietly shut the door and locked the truck. My brain and heart were racing. Was that a dying cow? No. A pissed off bear? No way. A coyote of some sort? Not a chance. Rabbits in distress make creepy noises. Yeah, but not with the volume that thing had. What about an elk bugle? Man, that doesn't sound like any elk I've seen or heard on nature shows. Cougar's make terrible noises, but I've heard them in the woods and on nature shows, it wasn't that.

That scream scared me so bad; I slept in my truck. I was so afraid; I couldn't even leave the vehicle to grab my sleeping bag from my tent. I pulled out the silver emergency blanket from my glove box and put on all the jackets I had in the cab. I put my keys in the ignition in case I needed to leave in a hurry and left my boots on. It wasn't the best night sleep I've ever had.

My feathered research subjects proved to be difficult to find in the Mount Shasta area. This mountain is steeped in mysteries that I was unaware of at the time. I thought the area just gave me a creepy feeling. But I know it wasn't just in my head. At that time of year, the snow line was still blocking vehicles from the higher vista points and specifically the campgrounds near Panther Meadow. Yeah, it is literally named after the mountain lion.

Well aware of the name, I carefully headed down the logging road covered in snow towards the meadow, searching for tracks in the snow. I must have looked like a life-sized bobblehead, looking up into the trees and back to the snow with every couple of steps. I had to park about a mile from Panther Meadow. Halfway to the meadow, I suddenly realized the bird chatter had stopped. Pausing, I strained my ears.

What is that noise?

Behind me, coming up the road was the sound of dogs. Big dogs.

I scrambled up the snowy bank alongside the road I was navigating and found a tree to strategically hide behind. The excited barks grew louder. Now I could hear their heavy panting as they neared. One dog, no now two, three, five, six dogs…those are wolves!!! This was not a group of huskies; these were freaking wolves that could make Marmaduke look like their sibling!

What in the hell are wolves doing here?

Remember, this was 2002, long before the reintroduced wolves in the upper U.S. made their way into central Oregon.

At this point, I was feeling really small and unarmed. Do I head back the way I came; in the opposite direction the wolves had gone? What if they back tracked? Do I go away from this road and head back, paralleling it at a distance?

Wait, more noise coming from the direction of my truck. People. This was people. They slowly came into view. Two men and a woman. As they came closer, I realized they were dressed in authentic looking Native American clothing. Rough leather pants and jackets.

I yelled hello down to them and slid down the snow to intercept them.

"Oh man. I just saw a pack of wolves run past, we have to get out of here," I said excitedly. The trio looked at me strangely. I guess I did pop out of nowhere.

"Those are our dogs," one of the men said.

"What? Those are wolves' man, they came up to my waist," I exclaimed.

"We will leave. Stand here," the man pointed behind him and next to the slope. The other man let out the loudest whistle I have ever heard. We all just waited in silence.

After what seemed like an eternity of weirdness, I could hear the wolves coming. I began to squirm a little. The men had handguns in waist holsters, but still, what the hell are these guys thinking?

The wolves or dogs or whatever they were, rounded the bend, tongues lolling bright red from their mouths. They barely even acknowledged us and sped past us and disappeared around the next bend.

My eyes must have been as big as dinner plates. The only man to speak looked at me, "See. Half wolves."

I stared at him incredulously.

Without another word, the trio looked down at the ground in front of them and shuffled through the snow after the wolf dogs.

I was dumbfounded. I watched them disappear around the bend and then I sat in the snow. I was at a loss. Following them didn't make a lot of sense and I needed to check out Panther Meadow before the day got any later. Shaking my head, I got up and began back down the road towards the meadow.

Arriving at the meadow, I began to relax a bit. It had been a while since I ran into those out of time people and their "pets". The meadow was also beautiful. I relaxed and began to explore around, searching for the telltale sign of my woodpeckers. After about an hour, I was standing near the center of the meadow when every hair on my body stood on end. This was fight or flight. I spun around in a quick 360. Nothing.

I backed up against a tree and just watched my surroundings. Something was definitely watching me and it was a predator.

I decided it was time to go. I cut across the open area so I could see anything following me. Once I neared the tree line that would take me back to the road I came in on, I found the likely culprit. Not the deer tracks in the snow, but the mountain lion tracks paralleling the deer. They were from that day, so fresh for sure.

Cougars love to get up in a tree or on a high rock and ambush their prey. Jump down and break the animal's neck. It was a long way back to my truck and I made sure not to walk anywhere near a tree on the way back.

My ghost encounter in Costa Rica was scary. But nothing could prepare me for a night on Snow Mountain north of San Francisco. That night was straight out of a horror movie.

This excursion found me and my thesis advisor in a very remote part of the state. This particular Snow Mountain (there are a lot around the country) is on the southern end of the North Coast Range. From the mountain top where we camped that night, we could see the Pacific Ocean in the distance. The view was breathtaking, and we enjoyed the sunset while eating our sandwich dinner. I had nearly stepped on a rattlesnake earlier in the day, so we were exhausted from the scare and all the unsuccessful hiking we had done searching for woodpeckers. Add to that the road up here was rock scree with no trees and thousands of feet straight down if you went over the side of the one-way forest road to get up here.

Our tents were setup next to the truck forming a crescent shape. We had no fire as we always retired with sunset and rose with the sun. Firewood and campfires were more trouble than they were worth.

We were talking about our plan for the next day as the full moon began to light our surroundings. The sun had dipped below the ocean on the horizon. Then suddenly, clouds from the ocean began to blow past us. Not over us, but due to our high elevation the clouds swirled around us. Chunks of cloud the size of small cars, or big ghosts blew between us as we watched. It reminded me of the spooky fog in an Evil Dead movie. Yeah, that was enough for us, we went to our tents and crashed from fatigue.

Just as I had fallen asleep, I was jolted awake by something. The wind had stopped, and the forest was silent.

What had woken me up and why is all the hair on my body standing on end?

CRUNCH.

What the fuck was that? I screamed in my head.

CRUNCH.

I strained my ears to the point of rupturing in an attempt to determine the location and reason for that sound.

CRUNCH.

It was the sound of pine needles being walked on. But it was slow and methodical…bipedal. No way a bear or deer or mountain lion makes that noise. The deer hooves are too small, and they weigh too little. The bear and cougar have padded feet, they have to as predators. There is no way it is a person; we haven't seen another human for two days!

CRUNCH.

The footsteps had started on the far side of my companion's tent. The creature walked slowly around his tent, past my tent, and then stopped on the other side of my pickup truck. I strained my ears so hard. I held my breath. I was so afraid I didn't move or blink inside my tent.

After whom knows how long, I finally passed out. I don't know if it was from the fatigue of the day, fear of the event, or if I held my breath so long that I blacked out.

The next morning, I asked my research partner if he had heard anything strange in the night. He had not. I put it down in my research journal as a possible Bigfoot encounter. But if Sasquatch is a flesh and blood unknown primate, how did it stay still for so long after the last step that I heard? How did it not move until after I eventually fell asleep?

CHAPTER 38

ANOTHER PSYCHIC

JUNE 8, 2023

This proved to be no ordinary psychic. If any psychic can be ordinary.

Kathy Marjorie was a woman with an extraordinary ability to project her consciousness to a particular place and time to view things you have questions about. She has even helped solve over sixty missing person cases. While I didn't have any missing person issues, I had quite a few past experiences that I wanted her to view and provide information about. Things that I have vague memories of but little clarity.

"Okay, first off, I like to scan my client's chakras to see how they look and look for any physical or etheric implants." Kathy was a no-nonsense kind of older woman.

"Sounds good," I responded.

"Okay, hmmm, you have a really strong protective field around you. Are you aware of that?" I blinked and shook my head.

"Something or someone has your back. Okay, your Etheric Astral Body is orange gold in color. Let's look at your chakras. Good, looks like you have done work with your chakras. Your heart chakra has a lot of colors coming from it, it is just bleeding out of you into your surroundings. Most of your other chakras are free from blockage. Although your third eye is a little calcified. You could focus on opening that up more."

"Okay," I said, furiously scribbling notes.

"And your throat chakra is open in the back but blocked in the front."

"Can you tell why it would be blocked," I asked.

She squinted her closed eyes a little tighter. "Two ETs put a block about 2 inches in front of your throat chakra."

I nearly fell out of my chair. "Uh, wow. For months now, when I meditate, I have a tightness that arises in the left side of my throat in the front. It really bugs me, and I was worried I might have a plaque buildup in my vein on that side or something. Although, I'm under the impression you wouldn't be able to feel that. Regardless, it bugs me when I meditate."

"Nope, nothing medical. I asked if they could remove the blockage, but they said it is not time to speak the knowledge that you have locked away. These ETs are about five feet tall and wearing robes." She paused for a moment. "You are traveling at night, a lot. Astral traveling to attend trainings and classes."

"Let's see. I'm going to scan for implants now." She paused again. "I don't see anything active. I can see where there was a physical implant in your nose that was removed. Did you remove that?"

I blinked, dumbfounded. "No. But you know, in my teens and twenties I had bloody noses pretty much every night. Then in my later twenties it just stopped and hasn't happened since."

"Yeah, the nose implants are fairly common. Looking at you I see there was something from past lives showing on your heart and in your brain. Those are ancient. Wow, you signed up for all the feels, didn't you?"

I laughed nervously, "I guess."

"Okay, now what did you want me to remote view?" Kathy asked.

I went on to explain the time I had something walk around my tent in the North Coast Range of California but made sure not to lead her. "Okay, in May of 2002, I was camping in California, in the coast range north of San Francisco. Something happened. Can you see that for me?"

"Yep, give me a second to travel there." I had gotten used to her pauses by this point. "You said at night, right?" I nodded. She closed her eyes again. "Was it a full moon?"

"Yes, I believe it was." I remember how creepy it was once it got dark and the shadows the full moon had cast.

"I see a truck and two tents and your aura. Yeah, juvenile Sasquatch. He came through a portal to check you out. Walked around your camp and then back out another portal. He was curious. He saw your light through the forest and came in to see what you were."

There it was. Confirmation of what I felt that night. Confirmation of what my higher self-answered during my QHHT session. Sasquatch is real and they can travel through portals. No wonder their tracks pop up out of nowhere and disappear just as easily. And that no trigger-happy hunter has ever bagged one.

"What's next?" Kathy asked nonchalantly. She must be so used to the Wooniverse after decades of her own encounters and doing readings for others.

"Wow. Okay, same timeframe, over at Mount Shasta on the south side. I stayed in a campground for two nights. There was something odd about my time there. I was uncomfortable on the mountain and came down to the base on the south side to camp for two nights, which was unusual for me. I rarely stayed in campgrounds."

Kathy closed her eyes again. "Two tall men in red robes with hoods materialized outside your tent. They are mountain beings. They live in the mountain. They sent a telepathic message to you asking you to come out of your tent. You come out of your tent and ask them, "who are you guys?" I can see you conversing with them, but they noticed me. They can see that my astral form is there. They are letting me see but not hear your conversation. I am getting that you are connected to these mountain people. They are ancient and immortal. Seems like they are from the Andromeda Galaxy."

At this point, I'm just trying to get everything out before my time expires. I'm not even giving myself the chance to be awed. Thirty-minute sessions fly by. "Alright. In the early 1990's, I would wake up punching the wall in my bed. I lived in Central California in the farmland at the base of the Sierra Nevada Mountains, between San Francisco and L.A."

After a pause. "Yeah, I found you. I see a craft in front of your house. The lights around the outside of the craft are really bright." I had purposely left out the fact that sometimes I would wake and think how the streetlight seemed too bright before rolling over and going back to sleep. "These beings have a strong connection to your solar plexus. To previous lifetimes of yours. They have uniforms. Red with an insignia. These are not typical grays by any means. They are really old and wrinkled. I don't know what they are."

"Damn," I muttered. "Okay, there was many times in the 2000's where I drove from L.A. to my parent's house and I wouldn't remember the two and a half hours drive in the southern part of the Central Valley. I would just come to as I pulled into my parent's driveway."

"Let me see...I see you sometimes in that same white truck but sometimes in a blue SUV."

"Yeah, I had both those trucks during those years," I confirmed. Damn she is good. "First the blue 4-Runner and then I sold it for the white pickup."

"Well, I see a gigantic craft over the valley. Like, really huge. I see your entire vehicle being pulled up into the craft. You remain calm and beings take you from the vehicle and lead you to a room on the ship where you meet with these tall, robed beings. You know them and have no fear. You are calm. You sit with them and relate your life experiences to them. They seem to listen very intently on what you are sharing."

"Can you describe the beings? Do you know who they are?"

"They are very tall, with robes. They have elongated faces, human like. They have very dark skin. Very wrinkly skin. Almost like tree bark. They are very wise. Wise and ancient. They keep calling you "Ambassador". I think they are the same as Mount Shasta. There are not a lot of people on Earth like you at this time. But I don't know who these beings are, I've never seen them before."

I knew Kathy had been researching UFOs for around forty years. The idea that she had not encountered this type of ET intrigued me. "So, considering how many ETs you have seen, it is pretty unique for you to come across a new race?" I asked.

"Oh yeah, I've been at this for a long, long time and I have never seen these beings."

CHAPTER 39

CONTACT, PART 2?

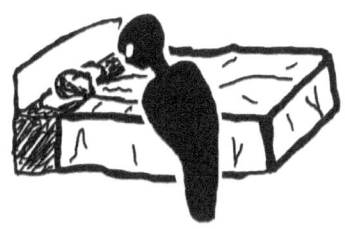

A week later, I was struggling through restless sleep. Dreaming again was something I was not used to after around two decades of not remembering dreams. I don't mean waking and forgetting, I mean waking and thinking that I didn't dream at all.

In the middle of that night, I woke from a dream of interacting with an unknown woman, but I couldn't remember what we were doing or discussing. We were out in public somewhere. I went back to sleep.

Sometime later, I woke from a dream where I was outside and an orange orb in the sky gently floated back and forth in front of my home. I rolled over and returned to sleep.

Later, I woke to a chill along my back. It was so reminiscent of my ghost girl encounter in Costa Rica that I immediately thought I was being visited by a specter. As my senses came online, I realized that I was paralyzed. Lying on my side, I strained my neck to look up and behind me. There, standing in the dark of my bedroom was the shadow form of a being. It had to be about seven feet tall. It had an enlarged head and elongated arms. It was leaning over the bed looking at me. In the span of seconds, I wondered if it was an astral projection before I tried to kick back with everything I had. I was still paralyzed.

Suddenly the paralysis in my leg gave out and I kicked straight back with my foot. The being vanished. Strangely, I immediately fell asleep again. But how? I should have jumped out of bed freaking out and woke my wife over it. But no, just blink and I was out cold.

In the morning, I went over the event in my head. I couldn't believe I finally had physical contact that I could remember and instead of asking its name, I kicked at it!

After nightfall that same day, I took the dogs out. Same routine as always. One last time out to pee before everyone prepped for bed.

While watching the sky, I saw a bright orange flash in the sky. Then to the right of that I saw the same flash again. It suddenly struck me this orange thing was just like my dream the night before of an orange orb drifting back and forth in the sky in front of my house.

CHAPTER 40

THE REPTILIAN

JUNE 21, 2023

My wife was at the hospital weekly at this point in her battle with cancer. Life was brutal for her, and I struggled to keep up with work and our kids needs while trying to keep her as comfortable as possible.

One afternoon, during a procedure, she asked me to go over a few blocks from the hospital to a bubble tea joint. I was glad to escape the hospital and all the feelings of dread that I pick up from other people in stressful situations. Being empathic can be brutal if you don't know how to shield yourself properly before leaving the house.

I was halfway to the restaurant when I crossed a street where the sidewalk was empty. I know it was empty; I had looked both ways, scanning for cars and the sidewalk for pedestrians. The buildings along this section also lacked store fronts. Not even the presence of any employees only doors.

Out of nowhere, I heard behind me the tell-tale sound of heels clicking on the sidewalk. It was loud enough, that my first impression was a woman in high heels. At the same time, I took notice, I got the strongest hit of dread that I could remember ever having. Whoever was behind me had a brutal aura they were projecting. I started to wonder if I was being followed by a witch or some kind of demon in human form.

I reached a building with windows along its length. I tried desperately to look at the windows to see who was stalking me. Without success.

I sped up my gait. At the next driveway to a parking lot, I cut left and headed up a new sidewalk. Whatever was behind me turned and followed me. At this point my heart was racing frantically. It was fight or flight dread just like those days camping twenty years ago.

The clicks of the shoes changed cadence as the walker moved into the parking lot and came along to parallel me. As it pulled even with me, I turned and looked. A loud voice in my head screamed, "Reptilian!"

The shoe clicker was a guy. I was stunned. I am 6'2" and this guy was a few inches taller than me. He had hard-soled shoes that were making the clicks. Expensive denim jeans, a sleeveless t-shirt, bleached blonde hair, huge muscular arms covered in tattoos, and dark sunglasses. If ever there was a Reptilian masquerading as a human, it had to be this guy.

I slowed my pace to see where he was going. Reaching the next street at the end of this parking lot, he just walked out into heavy traffic to reach the other side. A car slammed on his breaks and honked at him. The guy didn't even seem phased and kept going.

Heart still racing, I changed my direction towards my drink destination. "What the hell was that?" I muttered to myself.

This chapter might lose a lot of readers, and fair enough as it seems totally insane. However, there are a lot of esoteric instances of reptilian beings around the planet and throughout time. Egypt has the Crocodile god Sobek and the snake goddess Widget. Abrahamic religions have the talking serpent from the garden of Eden. Asia has the wise beings with a human upper body and snake lower body called the Naga. In Buddhism, the serpent Mucalinda is the protector of Buddha. Central American mythology has Mixcoatl known as the Cloud Serpent and father of Quetzalcoatl depicted with snake imagery himself.

So, did all these cultures across time and space on Earth come up with the same idea of magical and powerful beings with human and snake/reptile forms? Or, as many in UFOlogy would say, are there ETs or inter dimensional beings that are reptilian in form but can assume human form through mental capabilities that seem like magic or perhaps with technology that projects an image of humans?

Before my awakening, I was on the fence with the idea of whether dragons had really existed in the past on Earth and the possibility of reptilian humanoids existing somewhere in the universe. However, the more I research UFOlogy and the claims of contact with ETs, the more I opened up to the idea of reptilians. Especially, when viewing mythology around the world and the aspect that the gods were really ETs along the idea of Ancient Astronaut theories via Erich von Daniken. The easiest way to access these theories is through the HISTORY Channel's *Ancient Aliens* show.

In a nutshell, the Ancient Astronaut theory looks at all the ancient history mythologies and depictions of the "gods" and looks for aspects that match today's technology. For example, many ancient cave and wall art around the world depicts bizarre entities that look like ETs. Many of them even look like they are wearing helmets protecting against the environment the same way our NASA astronauts must wear helmets with oxygen in outer space. The astronaut glyph in the Nazca Desert, the Hopi cave drawings of Kachinas, the sarcophagus lid of the Mayan ruler Pacal the Great, and the astronaut suit-wearing Dogu figures of prehistoric Japan just to name a few. Then there is the Chapter 1 of the Book of Ezekiel where he pretty much describes some sort of airship or UFO appearing before him.

CHAPTER 41

A WARNING

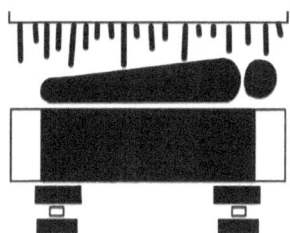

JUNE 24, 2023

It was three days later when I next meditated. I had that similar, someone has a message feeling all morning.

Once I was deep into my meditative mental state, a tan-colored Reptilian came to me. I pushed it away and returned to the blank movie screen I focus on before my consciousness is led somewhere.

Eventually, I found myself confronted by my blue ET Ascended Master guide. At some point, I really need to figure out his name.

He guided me to my Spirit Command Center. Once inside, I went to the room with all my guides. I asked Crabby if he could give me a healing. I laid down on a table and an ET and my Snow Leopard Feline humanoid guide came in to heal me. Next, my Mother Goddess guide came and held my right hand. The Snow Leopard placed a golden triangle over my head.

After the healing was complete, I exited the room with my guides and returned to the hallway. Then for the first time, I noticed a second floor in this grand gallery. Up at the second story level, was one of my Guardian Angels standing on a balcony. That was strange.

Next, I felt myself drawn up to the far end of the hall where my Watcher Angel waits. I flew into the Watcher and suddenly appeared inside a technological room. I had teleported to a ship of some kind. I was perfectly calm as I believed I had been to this ship many times. Usually there were three ETs of different races waiting to greet me in this room with the large window or screen that viewed Earth. But this time they were absent.

I turned away from the view and was confronted by tan Reptilian.

I think I blinked in amazement to see him on the ship. My two Feline Guards, the Snow Leopard and the African Lion, were standing on either side of me and slightly in front. They were clad in their usual armor with their tall spears up at attention.

Much braver than I had been on the street with that evil Reptilian in human form, I approached this Reptilian and blasted him with love energy from my heart chakra. I could see rainbow colors gushing from my chest and smacking that being in his chest. The beautiful technicolor aura washed over his scales and enveloped his muscular upper body that was clad in medieval style armor in the same fashion as my Feline Guards. To my shock, the Reptilian being didn't budge. He just took the barrage calmly.

This display should be showing me he wasn't evil, but I had to be sure. I walked forward and the seven foot tall being went down on one knee and bowed his head. I placed my right hand on his left shoulder and blasted him with a more furious wave of love, acceptance, and appreciation for his existence. Again, he failed to budge.

196

I stepped back and my Feline Guards went to flank the Reptilian, facing him like prison guards. It seemed an uneasy truce.

Suddenly, my dragon, Ragnar, in a shrunken down draconian form appeared behind me and put his hand on my shoulder. I had never seen him take a different form, but he looked similar to the Reptilian we were confronting. Then I realized that behind him were my Guardian Angel entourage in their black or white hooded robes.

"I am here to warn you that you are in danger," said the Reptilian, speaking for the first time.

Ragnar and my Felines warned him that he was the only one in danger here. "He has nothing to worry about, he has our protection and that of an entire Spiritual Army behind him." I wasn't sure which of the Feline guards had communicated that since it was all telepathy.

I got the impression that this Reptilian was closer to a dragon than a lower-level Reptilian like the one I had seen on the street. Maybe that meant he lived at a higher density than most Reptilian species?

It seemed his warning was finished, and he had nothing more to say. I turned to leave, and that Reptilian didn't make any move to stop us.

I wanted to see more of the ship. Just as that thought struck me, a being that reminded me of the Star Wars cantina scene with the human body and planarian-like brown head appeared to guide me around. The unique fellow led us down a hall to a grand gallery of some kind. Something told me this was the seat of the Galactic Federation. It also made sense, I felt like I've been to this ship many times before. Maybe this is where I astral travel at night?

I wanted to use a MedBed in hopes of lessoning the daily nerve pain I lived with. The guide took me down another hallway. This ended in a circular room with doors everywhere. There must have been at least a dozen doors in this room.

I went to the center door and there was a bed that looked incredibly similar to a tanning bed. I got in and the top automatically lowered down over me. Scores of lights began to flash and flicker as the machine hummed. Then I was shocked to see Crabby appear and work the controls on the lid of the bed.

Once it was finished, I left with my entourage, and we reappeared back in my Spirit Command Center.

These deep meditation interactions melt my brain. Am I losing my mind? Would I have been tossed in an insane asylum if I had lived 50 years earlier? What terrible lives awakened people had to live in the 1900s. Well hell, any time really. Isn't it the same as being burned as a witch?

CHAPTER 42

THE TREATMENT IS WORSE THAN THE CURE

JUNE 26, 2023

My wife's cancer battle wore on. She was exhausted and sick from the chemotherapy. I was physically exhausted from keeping the house and business running and mentally exhausted from watching her deteriorate.

Once a week, we trudged to the Cancer Center so she could receive her treatment. I quickly learned that I had to put up a shield around me before entering or I would be emotionally sickened from the pain and grief that roils inside that building, and all hospitals like it.

Anyone that has gone through or helped someone with chemo can attest to the little rituals at the beginning. Last bathroom trip. Getting out snacks. Finding the ice machine. Getting out a book or iPad.

Once Jennifer was settled and her IVs were running, I focused on what I felt the need to do on these visits. I put on my headphones and some meditation music. I went through my meditation spin up as usual.

Only on these occasions, once I had all my chakras engaged, I returned to my heart and focused on it. I would make sure I connected to Source and had my yellow tether running down from Source to my crown chakra. I made sure the energy I was about to share was from Source and not my energy directly.

For who knows how long, I would spin my heart chakra and its rainbow colors until the chakra ball was the size of a basketball. Then I would envision myself squeezing the ball down to the size of a baseball. Dense and tight, then exploding the energy out from my chest. I pictured the energy exploding out in every direction to reach the people in the Cancer Center.

Patients, family support, and the employees. I couldn't imagine working in a place like that and having to see patient after patient battling for their very lives.

CHAPTER 43

THE NOTORIOUS STASIS TUBES

On this day, I tried something a little different.

Before beginning my meditation, I politely informed Archangel Michael and Raphael that I wanted to re-activate my psychic abilities. Once that intention was in place, I went through my normal protocols at start.

While staring at my blank movie screen in my mind's eye to clear my perception, I felt pulled out of my inner movie theater. I appeared inside my Spirit Command Center. Again, I felt pulled, this time towards the first door on the left, the realm with my Soul Tree. Every time I enter this room, I see myself in my child form from this life. My brother and sister Soul Echoes were holding hands around our Soul Tree, but I did not join them. Instead, I breathed in the Source energy that enters the top of the tree, into the leaves, down the branches of the tree to the trunk and then out to each Soul Echo surrounding the tree. It always reminded me of the scene from Ghostbusters when Gozer blasted Rick Moranis and Sigourney Weaver with the energy beams.

Oddly enough, I felt charged and returned to the Hall. I strolled down the corridor past the many tables aligned down the center of the great room and stopped before one long enough to tap the crystal ball resting on it.

Poof!

I found myself floating in space. Only, I wasn't me. I was some kind of non-human entity wearing a space suit of some kind. I looked down at my hand and counted four fingers encased by a body suit. Somehow, I knew my skin was gray blue, my head was bald, and it was slightly larger than 'normal' along with my eyes. But not the grotesquely oversized head people depict the little grays with.

Before I could wonder what was next, a massive spaceship floated into view and lit me up with a bright tractor beam like in Star Trek. As the beam pulled me towards the ship and what I assumed was a cargo bay, I marveled at its massiveness. Once inside the structure, I could not help but be reminded of the Empire in Star Wars. There were smaller ships and stacked futuristic looking crates all around the massive bay. The Empire comparison didn't end there. Awaiting me patiently were hundreds of beings that looked the same as my current ET form, lined up at attention like a military force.

A being of more senior appearance wearing a military-type uniform greeted me. And then led me past the assembled soldiers. They all watched me glide past. I really felt like I was someone of import. But why had I been floating around in space by myself?

The other being led me to a MedBed that looked strikingly like the one I had seen on the Federation ship. Lying inside the device, the bright lights reappeared. Only this time they were very focused. Different portions of my body were individually blasted with light. First my eyes and ears. My stomach, then liver and gall bladder. I got the impression this was a healing in exchange for awakening but that seemed odd if I was this ET and not Matt the Earthling.

Next, I was taken to a sprawling room with hundreds of stasis tubes. I don't know how I knew they were stasis tubes, but they looked like stasis tubes from any of dozens of sci-fi movies out there. Some of the tubes had beings just like my current ET self, others were empty. In the center of the room stood a marble looking pillar with a device that looked like an eye. I reached out and took the device. It instantly transported me to somewhere in the upper Atlantic Ocean, to a Space Ark.

What the hell is a Space Ark and how do I know I'm in the Atlantic Ocean?

I found myself in a room with a big table. I could see a floating hologram of Earth. The hologram showed markers around the planet. I got the impression these showed the locations of other Space Arks like the one I was in now.

My concentration was jarred by the appearance of human men coming in from my right. I felt like the energy was a psychic attack to keep me out and disrupt me. It caused me to slip out of my meditation and shift back into my home and human body.

These super vivid events leave me with more questions than answers.

Much later, I would discover the idea of Space Arks while listening to a podcast by Dr. Michael Salla called *Exopolitics Today*. Dr. Salla has been exploring the UFO phenomenon and interviewing experiencers and whistleblowers for decades. One gentleman that Dr. Salla has interviewed many times over multiple years is a man claiming to be an Army insider that completes missions related to UFO's and ETs. This man goes by JP. One of his missions was to a Space Ark in the Atlantic Ocean.

It is a long story, but it seems that at a very ancient time in Earth's history, an unknown ET race deposited these massive spaceships or Arks, around the planet. Various governments around the planet have been uncovering these Space Arks and making progress with studying the interiors.

Is JP telling the truth? Is it one of these Space Arks I found my astral ET form inside?

I just don't have the answer for any of this, but it was a fascinating correlation to discover months later on the *Exopolitics Today* podcast.

CHAPTER 44

REOCCURRING THEMES

At this point, I had worked with seven or eight psychics to sort out my metaphysical life. A few of them more than once, and with Gabby, maybe ten times. Something about Gabby's energy really resonated with me. We must have lived lives as the same ET race or something. Some soul contract for this life maybe?

A couple of practitioners just didn't resonate with me, while the others did. But regardless of that, there were a few things that all these people picked up on and I had seen mirrored in my meditations.

- *I am a healer, maybe something with sound.*
- *Pyramids are portals for travel, energy creators, communications devices, and healing facilitators.*
- *I was a wizard or alchemist in multiple past lives and killed for it, usually by the church.*
- *I am supposed to teach or lecture; but what, I haven't a clue.*

- *Lots of astral traveling at night, explains why I'm exhausted every morning.*
- *Something to do with timelines.*
- *Mantid beings and Antares.*
- *Throat chakra.*
- *I need to find my Tribe. I had to stop hiding and paying psychics.*

I don't feel like a healer. And while I love music, I failed miserably at trying to learn guitar and I think I might be tone deaf.

Considering the number of times I have seen myself living a life as a wizard in regressions and meditations, and all the dragon stuff, that makes sense. All the times I was killed by the church also makes sense why all organized religions trigger me in a negative way.

Teaching something doesn't make sense. I already had my spat with teaching college biology and won't ever go back to that. Especially, with AI basically writing college kids reports for them.

I've been told I astral travel at night to take classes, to do training, to plant trees, or to work in my alchemy shop.

Timelines are mind numbing. I believe there are almost unlimited numbers of timelines, but just trying to understand how they work melts my brain. And the fact that every psychic I've met with brings up my working with timelines is just plain crazy to me. Which is comical when I consider all the other 'crazy' things I've experienced.

The Mantid that comes to me in some meditations is fascinating. It never speaks or uses telepathy with me. However, it always shows me different shapes. Almost like the being's language is shapes. I don't know.

My throat chakra annoys the hell out of me. If I don't get deep in a meditation, the pressure on my throat doesn't arise. But every single time my meditation goes deep, that crushing sensation of pressure on the left side of my throat rears its ugly head.

My Tribe. Well, I have been a loner my whole life. I've always only had a couple of good friends at a time, and I haven't made any new friends since college. I did find it funny to have a psychic tell me that Spirit says I can't keep paying psychics, that I must find my Tribe!

But how crazy is it that a half dozen professional psychics over two years and my own meditations share the same list of running themes?

.

CHAPTER 45

I'VE HAD ENOUGH

MOO

Two years' worth of crushing pressure on my left throat during meditations was enough. I was going to fix this today, no excuses.

I had been anxious all day leading up to this meditation. I literally felt like I was going to pop out of my skin.

Once I had gotten deep into meditation, I felt pulled from Earth out into orbit. While floating around in space, comedic nightmare fuel reared its ugly head. If you have seen the South Park episode where Cartman is kidnapped by Zeta grays and a satellite is implanted in his butt, then you know where I am coming from. If you haven't seen it, then look it up!

Floating in space before me was that same South Park art stylized Zeta Gray ET staring at me. Not as creepy as Whitley Streiber's *Communion* book cover, but creepy and comedic combined. Then a leopard Feline being appeared next to the Zeta. Man, you'd think I had done shrooms before this session!

Next, I found myself in my Spirit Command Center, specifically in my spirit team room. A little shook up, I took a seat at the desk that sits away from the massive table the spirits sit around. Think King Arthur's Round Table only big enough for over a hundred human ancestors, ETs, Animal Spirits, and more to all sit around comfortably.

I looked across the room at everyone assembled. "Team and my Ego, I am ready to remove the blocks," I said.

The Eagleman got up from his chair and came to me first. He stood in front of me and waved his wings back and forth in a mesmerizing dance of feathered furls. Next, Mother Goddess came and hugged me. Then Crabby came behind me. He always seemed to do his healing on me from behind.

Finally, I stood and floated to the center of the table so all my guides could surround me. Then my corporeal throat began to tighten more than it normally did during deep meditations.

I asked the two ETs to remove my throat chakra block. They appeared before me and seemed to work on it. Touching the front of my throat with their spindly fingers. My physical throat tightened even more. If I didn't know better, I would swear Darth Vader was in my room choking me out with the Force.

With my eyes still closed, I reached out onto my desk. With my right hand, I wrapped my fingers around my green quartz crystal ball. My left hand grabbed my large Orgone pyramid and lifted it into the air. I manipulated the pyramid until I was grasping the bottom with the top pointed away from my hand and towards me. Without understanding why, I did it, I jammed the point of the pyramid into my throat. Right on the left side where the pressure was always felt.

I began to hum loudly as I dug the pyramid into my neck. No idea why I was humming.

I twisted it around. *Up, Up, Down, Down, Left, Right, Left, Right, B, A, Start.* Sorry, bad video game joke for Gen X'ers.

The pain between the tightness of my throat and the pressure of a sharp point digging into my neck was intense. Eventually, the tight feeling drifted away. At the same time, I saw the vision of a butterfly and then a phoenix birth into fiery life!!!

I was sweaty when I finally left my meditation and put the pyramid down. I'm glad to say that since that day, I have never had the throat tightness again. I don't know if it was asking to remove the block on my throat chakra, or the humming, or the physical jabbing with the pyramid that cleared it. Maybe it took all three?

CHAPTER 46

TIME LINES

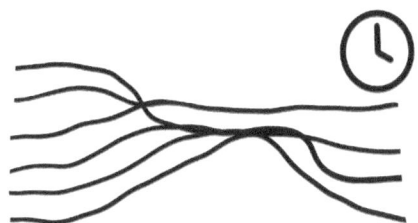

AUGUST 8, 2023

Gabby Lyon proved to be my go-to psychic. I just resonate with her and love her energy in the same way that I get charged from talking to Bev Dovin, my QHHT practitioner.

We've worked together enough times that our sessions always start with pleasantries. But time is money, so we still get into it pretty quickly.

"Well, you know I always have questions, but I prefer to see where spirit is going to take us," I said. I must sound like a broken record to Gabby at this point.

"Yep, I know. Can I tell you that I have felt like drawing a Tarot card for you all morning?"

"Really? That is new. Let's do it." I honestly was excited about that as I've never had a Tarot reading before. "Do I need to do anything?"

"No, I'm just going to shuffle this deck, and you can set an intention.

Then when you have the intention, don't tell me just tell me you are ready."

"Okay." I thought about it for a second, but I quickly went to the intention of learning who my Star Family is or who has been visiting me. "Okay, I got it. Let's do this."

Gabby stopped shuffling and smiled. "Okay." She grabbed the top card and lifted it up to show me. Then craned her neck to see the card herself. "What a beautiful card. This is Angel Galactic Brother card. Piercing truth. The bottom here shows Earth elemental and Faith."

"Huh. Before I tell you what I wanted, let's go through the card," I said.

"Do you want me to read the book for this card or just go with my intuition and what I'm getting from spirit?"

"Spirit."

"Okay; You have a huge spirit team in this life to help you." In my QHHT, my Higher Self answered that I have 107 guides on my spirit team. "The Galactic Brother and you are Soul Fragments. He is bringing you into balance. All your soul fragments are coming online at the same time. I see a computer board with all the little circuits coming into the main chip. He is the main chip and you are one of the many circuits. You are not the Master Port. For the Galactic Brother, I'm getting Andromedin System, backside of the system, and Arcturian energy. Loyalty and family are corner blocks. The being is "Weaver"."

"That is the brother's name, Weaver?" I asked, furiously scribbling notes.

"Yes, I'm getting Weaver. Actually, Time Weaver. They are showing me lots of spheres, time is circular. You are having conversations with Time Weavers at night. I feel like if you look into your coffee in the morning, like sit with it and stare at the coffee. You might be able to retrieve some of the memories from the night before. Accept the consciousness stream."

"You're blowing my mind right now," I said in all seriousness.

"Time Weaver creates new timelines, new planetary systems. Testing time. Conjunctures. White crystal. Blueprint and creation. He focuses on knowledge and learning. Evolution and growing. I feel like he is 14th Density. I get the feeling of being very grounded, gold, brown, yellow. The Akashic Record system was created by Time Weaver. It allows beings that can access it to walk through time.

"You came here in this life to experience the time break and report back to them. Delicate changes. There are tiny tubules of timelines and the main chute down the center is the main timeline. Then leap into another sphere. You are taking in too much and it is straining your nervous system. Just trust the process.

"Time Weaver is saying you are an old soul, strong soul. They want you to go easy on yourself. When you need help, ask for help. Know you have served, there is no space for judgement."

I could feel pressure welling up in my chest. I think I was receiving the energy from Gabby that she was receiving from spirit. As if to confirm it, I could see Gabby shake her head and slump her shoulders.

"Whew…thank you for letting me share that with you," she said.

"No, thank you. That was intense," I said. We kind of just stared at each other for a few moments. The clock told me I was almost out of time. "Well, now that we did the fun stuff, I need to talk about something serious."

"Oh, okay."

"Um, it's hard to admit it but I have a drinking problem. I've drank a fair amount for decades, but the pandemic really caused me to fall down the rabbit hole. I've been drinking like three bottles of bourbon a week for a few years now. And I don't know if you know Kathy Marjorie, but she is great at health readings and she told me I had a problem with my liver and gallbladder. So, I'm wondering if we can look into that. Why can't I quit? I almost feel like I'm drinking in the evening to fall asleep to avoid something."

"Let's see. Give me a minute to feel into it," Gabby said. After a moment, "It isn't you. You have an attachment. I can see you in a dark place and the entity attached to you there. Lots of drinking there. Does that make sense to you?"

"Yeah. Probably at a bar or beer festival ten years or so ago."

"It is an entity. You will have to get it cleared if you haven't been able to do it on your own." Gabby looked genuinely concerned.

"Before this, I never believed the idea of attachments. But, for the last few years, I've heard a voice in my head, and I thought it was mine. When I was out of alcohol, I'd hear this voice say, *The liquor store is right next to the post office, you can get the mail and something to drink at the same time*. Like there was always an excuse to drink. If it was a hard day of work, have some drinks. Frustrating day with the kid's hockey, drink. Something to celebrate, have to have the drinks out."

"Yeah. Attachments are real. They are getting something from their host and whatever this thing is, it seems to love alcohol. I have gotten rid of attachments before, but it is not my specialty. I'm going to send you to Tilly von Lawrence. She is a good friend of mine and specializes in this kind of thing. I'll send an email to introduce you to her so she can get you in faster."

"Wow," I said. "Thank you so much."

"I'm sorry I can't do it for you right now, but if you want to clear it for good, Tilly is one of the best."

Later that day, I was waiting in the pickup line at the kid's school. The image of Savannah Cosman popped in my head. I don't know why because to my knowledge she was just a hypnotist and not a psychic that could remove evil entities. Plus, she was so busy her waiting list for QHHT sessions was more than two years out.

I looked up her website and scrolled around to see if there was anything new. Sure enough, she was doing a workshop in six months in Jupiter, Florida.

"I'm sure it is already sold out," I grumbled. But I clicked on the link anyways. It was still open! And it wasn't that expensive. Three days of past life regressions and some TAUK thing! I clicked the pay button without even asking my wife! Well, psychic's and spirit keep telling me I have to find my Tribe. Maybe I'll click with someone at this thing?

CHAPTER 47

SAY HELLO TO MY LITTLE FRIEND

Gabby was true to her word. The same day we spoke, she had me connected with Tilly and we were trying to figure out a time to work together. Unfortunately, she was traveling, and it would be about a week before we could speak. I was convicted to maintain the sobriety I had started eight days earlier. That was actually a long stretch for me.

The next day, I was anxious. I had slept little that night. I work from home, and late in the afternoon, the anxiety was eating me alive. I quit work early and went to my hobby room to just sit in my recliner. Sometimes I just sit and listen. See what comes up without meditating.

Fairly quickly, I felt an energy to my left and down towards the floor. The energy was disgusting. With my eyes still closed, I turned my head towards the energy. In my mind's eye, I could see a grotesque being that looked like the scary as hell aliens in that *Fire and Sky* movie about the abduction of Travis Walton in the 1970's. Travis didn't like how Hollywood dramatized some of the aspects of the movie. However, he has given many interviews over the decades, and it is worth searching out if you are unfamiliar with his story.

"Are you a spirit guide?" I asked aloud. It didn't take me long to realize that wasn't the case. "No, you are not. You are my attachment to alcohol."

I felt into the entity. I sensed that I had brought it upon myself. For some reason, back at that time, I needed to drink. Maybe I needed to quiet my mind before bed. Maybe I subconsciously wanted to delay my awakening of my psychic abilities? Who knows.

But, looking back on it, that day was a monumental choice. I could keep drinking and block a lot of psychic experiences and shorten my life. Or choose to accept my gifts and whatever Soul Mission I have setup for myself in this life and stick around as long as possible for my mission and my kids.

Understanding through my intuition that I had asked for this attachment; I sent the being gratitude. I thanked it for sharing its pain and experiences with me. I blasted it with love and gratitude from my heart chakra.

"Thank you for sharing with me. Now, you have to leave as I do not need or want you anymore. You are not allowed to ever return to me or anyone in my family."

Then I mentally pictured myself physically reached down and grabbed the entity. I stood up and in my mind's eye I drop kicked the beast over the tree line and off my property!

I never drank again and that night I slept sounder than I had in decades.

This also brings up the idea of generational trauma. My mother's mother and my father were functional alcoholics most of their lives.

Did my alcoholism come to me as a generational trauma?

Maybe. If it did, I hope with all my heart that I broke that ancestral trauma, and it will not impact my children or their children in the future.

CHAPTER 48

HIGH MAGIC AND DARK TIMES

At this point of my journey into the Wooniverse, meditating had become a lot more entertaining than television. I had changed. I just couldn't watch horror movies anymore and even blockbuster action movies held little appeal. If I sat to watch something that wasn't a documentary, it would be a comedy, or better yet a romantic comedy.

On this particular day, my meditation proved to reinforce the sense in me that the world of consciousness was wildly entertaining compared to contrived television shows.

I meditated in front of my blank movie screen in my mind until I was transported to my Spirit Command Center. I never know what to do when I first arrive. I usually stand in the doorway for a moment until I feel drawn to something.

This time, something new happened. I could see my one main

Guardian Angel, Jerome, standing up on a second story balcony. He stood in front of a newly appeared doorway. Jerome is the only Guardian Angel that doesn't hide behind a hood. He appears as an old man with a monocle. Like a spiritual Monopoly Guy.

I floated up to the balcony. The entrance wasn't a traditional doorway. More like a hole in the wall that looked like a purple Jello galaxy. Slowly, I came to realize that it was a portal to past lives. Wow, talk about an advantageous door to have!

I went through the door and found myself standing near a small village. The town had a medieval feel to it and the people meandering around had a peasant type of dress about them. I was not my normal self. My mid length wavy blonde hair was gone, replaced with longer black hair that was straight and stringy.

Was this Earth? I wondered.

The sounds of screaming and war drifted into my field of awareness. I know that sound too well from my many past life regressions.

Peasants ran from the nearby forest and road to seek shelter in the village. In the distance, I saw grungy men with swords and axes, dirty leather breastplates and rough wooden shields. Their clothing were dark shades of brown and black. I couldn't help but be reminded of marauding Vikings.

It seems I was a magician in this life. I turned away from the invaders and faced the village. Conjuring a yellow-colored see-through barrier, I enveloped the town like a half sphere. It was instinctive and more like the hand and arm swirls done by the magicians in the Dr. Strange movie than the Dungeons and Dragons style of reciting a spell. I didn't verbally say anything during the spell casting.

Presented with an unanticipated barrier, the army slowed their rush towards the village. Their leader walked up to the shield and tentatively reached out and poked it with his sword. It may have shimmered with a window quality, but it was a solid barrier. It was apparent they had never encountered anything like it. The leader slammed his sword down on the barrier and his men rushed forward to do the same.

The force field was a full sphere and went under the village. I felt afraid that the marauders might get through the shield, thus I lifted the village and the ground below it into the air. The sound of the soil and tree roots rendering during the separation was deafening. It scared the wits out of the invaders, and they stumbled over each other in their effort to run back from whence they came.

I floated the city off over the forest in the opposite direction. At the time the villagers were just as awestruck as their would-be pillagers.

When the army had been gone for some time, I returned the floating sphere to its rightful place in the ground and disintegrated the yellow shield. The whole thing frightened the villagers too much. Instead of being praised, I was vilified and cast out from the village.

I flew into the air like superman, traveling in the same direction as I had levitated the village. After some time whooshing past the tops of trees, I reached a meadow with a waiting dark gray and black-scaled dragon. It was not as big as Ragnar but a similar black, albeit missing the purple sheen Ragnar possessed.

The dragon quietly greeted me and I climbed on board his back. The beast of myth and lore leapt into the air with his powerful back legs. I felt he could sense my disappointment. Once past the treetops he beat his wings furiously to gain altitude. We flew to the northeast. There was a chain of mountains in that direction.

My real body was getting overheated and queasy. I pulled back my consciousness and ended the meditation.

August 14

Three days later I did a healing session with Gabby. She sang for me and I had the wildest encounter. Three amorphous beings came to heal me. They looked like human-shaped blobs with galaxies in their bodies. One entity was blue, one green, and one black. It was so bizarre.

Afterwards, we had a little bit of time for her to lean into spirit for me.

"You are looking for pieces of yourself. Searching for sacred knowledge that you had but lost in this life. I see you surrounded by hundreds of books. You are a wizard. You need to breathe. There is a layer of energy behind you being blocked. You need to breathe it through the back of your spine. Breathe in the energy. Integrate everything through your body." She paused for a moment. "And teach. You are a teacher; you need to teach."

First, I had not told her anything about that magical meditation from earlier in the week. Second, teach what? I wondered. I already tried the college teaching career and liked it but failed to land a full-time position.

"You need to know you won't be hurt again. You know more this time. Next time you meditate, ask a dragon to come in to tell you more about sorcery."

What the living hell? How is she getting this? I didn't tell her about that meditation with the dragon and the village. I don't ever do or say anything that might lead the psychic.

CHAPTER 49

NIGHTMARE FUEL

Stuff has gotten weird. On one hand, I'm much calmer with all the meditation. On the other, the stuff I see during meditations are crazy enough that I keep waiting for the paddy wagon from the insane asylum to pull up in front of my house.

I've also noticed that I can get deep into a Theta brain state a lot faster than a year ago. On this day, this meditation was more like a drug trip than most. Not that I partake in drugs, but I've seen the movies!

The first thing that came to me after my mind left my blank movie screen was an image of Wonder Woman!

But she was like a comic book, not like real life. It was wild. She was 3D but her colors were like classic comic book colors from the 1950s. Well, maybe she wasn't Wonder Woman, but she was a powerful Amazon from the lore. A strong female warrior with a metal breastplate and metal bracers on her wrist. I got the impression she was a representation of my wife. I must admit, Jennifer is strong as hell going through multiple surgeries, five months of chemotherapy and three more surgeries on the horizon.

In fact, I remember hearing stories of how the Amazon women would cut off one breast to be better at shooting a bow. My wife had to remove her breasts to battle this cancer, so it was a powerful vision for me.

Wonder Woman took me to a crystal castle. Lots of weird technicolor. It only got stranger from there. The wall around the castle was formed by huge beings. Like weird giants butted up against each other, shoulder to shoulder. Somehow, they meshed together well enough that the only way through their united front was the front gate. Their bodies reminded me of how seamless the stones at Machu Picchu blend together. The two giants on either side of the gate were holding their arms up and out away from the castle, forming a 'door'.

I was led through the gate and across a field, past some medieval looking houses and into the courtyard of the crystal castle. Once inside, I found a huge chessboard covering the courtyard. Next, I found myself standing as one of the board pieces. Wonder Woman went to an upper level on one side and on the other side was the freaking plastic Burger King guy! Then they started throwing Lawn Darts at me and the other people acting as board pieces. Remember those dangerous 'toys' from the 1980s?

Somehow, I survived the deadly barrage. Next, Wonder Woman took me to the castle dungeon. She led me to a prison cell and stepped aside. In it was Stephen King's *IT* evil clown! I freaking hate clowns. Always have.

I don't know what Spirit was trying to show me with this meditation, but I feel strongly that Jennifer was embodied by that Wonder Woman figure. Maybe the evil clown was cancer, and she had bested it?

CHAPTER 50

PORTALS, DRAGONS, AND...LYNYRD SKYNYRD?

OCTOBER 2, 2023

At this point, I believe strongly in portals. Doorways to other dimensions or through time, or both!

When I meditate and hit portals, I know I am going far back in time or some place in another galaxy or maybe dimension. I see portals as bright yellow circles behind my eyelids. They start small in front of one eye then quickly grow and are gone so that eye is looking at blackness again. Then a portal will start on the other eye and do the same. It is like I am physically moving through portals early in the meditation.

This meditation the portals lasted for so long, I knew I was going way back in time or space, further than I had ever done before.

I saw a stream surrounded by a field. Mountains were off in the distance, wrapping around the giant grassland to form a valley. The stream was flowing from left to right as I faced it.

I asked how long ago this was? In my head I heard the words, *100,000 years.*

Next, I asked who I was supposed to meet here? Then a dragon encroached from the distance. It appeared to be black, so I thought it was Ragnar. Which was odd because he usually comes to get me and takes me to where I need to go.

Nope, I was wrong, it is two dragons. As they drew closer, they pulled apart and it was easier to see the two different beasts. Eventually, I could see it was Ragnar and the same smaller dragon I saw in my meditation as a wizard.

The smaller dragon landed on the other side of the river from me. Ragnar maintained his altitude and circled above.

Agnir, that was this dragons name. I absorbed the information that 100,000 years ago on Earth, the dragons still roamed openly and interacted with the world. Later they would leave this plane of existence, but I was not told why or when it took place.

When I lived that life with Agnir, I was a protector, a magician, but I was vilified for my magic powers. Agnir told me that I must forgive the past humans so I can accept the powers again in my current incarnation.

I agreed that he was correct. Then Lynyrd Skynyrd's Free Bird began playing in my head! If I haven't mentioned it before, since my Awakening began, I sometimes wake up to song lyrics playing in my head or when I'm thinking hard about something. This is my guides trying to give me a message and others have spoken of similar experiences with random music popping into their head.

My body shot into the air. I could fly on my own!

Ragnar and Agnir flew around with me. Physically, I could feel my body back in my chair, growing nauseous from the whirling and twirling through the air. I've always been prone to motion sickness.

Agnir flew alongside me. I floated over onto his shoulders along his back and took a seat. I got the feeling this was very familiar, and it was like once more for old times' sake. Unfortunately, I continued to grow nauseous, and we proceeded to land.

I thanked Agnir for this experience and pulled out of the meditation and returned to my body.

That…was…wild!!!

CHAPTER 51

CRYSTAL PSYCHOMETRY

PSYCHOMETRY

The extra-sensory ability of the user to gain accurate historical information from an object or place by physically touching an object. Also known as token-object reading.

In a session with Gabby, she got the hit that I had a connection to crystals. Leaning into it, we uncovered the idea that there are many crystal cities buried around the world. For example, she got the impression that there is a massive crystal city hidden underground in Peru. Given all the weird ET stuff that comes out of Peru, I really don't doubt her hit on that. Add to that, I have felt pulled to Peru for most my life.

The take home message for me, was that I should be able to do psychometry with crystals. Gabby thought that if I worked with a crystal, I could tap into the crystal grid of the planet and gain knowledge that way. Even so far as to find a specific crystal that should be able to geolocate these underground cities. This was a fascinating message for me as I have been intrigued by the idea that there are beings living underground, Inner Earth beings. Which was magnified for me when I think back on all the weird feelings I had around Mount Shasta, decades before I had heard of the idea of Telos. Telos is believed to be the underground city of advanced beings or survivors of Mu or Atlantis.

It didn't take me long to find out that crystal psychometry is very real. At this point, I've worked with dozens of crystals of all types and sizes. Initially, I would get little spurts of information. I would just see a stream of jarring images that were unrelated and then they would stop. But after some time, I began to get long, detailed image streams that were coherent. Here is one of the more interesting sessions that I have had.

(Phrases in "quotes" is me questioning the crystal; Phrases in *italics* are answers heard in my head; Underlined words are the images that I am seeing in my mind's eye)

Large Labradorite Crystal

My intention for this session was "Show me an underground crystal city".

First, I see a crescent and boomerang shape. I have seen this before, it is almost like a badge or emblem. The crescent faces downwards and the boomerang points down underneath the crescent. Then images begin to stream.

Mummy / Underground / Egyptian (I can see a square tunnel through solid rock. The rock is dark gray.)

Bird or Owl talon / Light (I can feel eyes watching me.)

Some kind of reptile bones like fossils. "Dinosaur??"

Stuck in Time

Witch hat / Magic / Dry region with dinosaur bones

Stuck in Time

Geologic layers of rock / Elbow / Bend / River (I can see a river in a dry region following a cliff on one side, the cliff bends and the river matches it. Lots of layers in the cliff face.)

Massive UFO.

"When?" - *Long time ago*

"Am I connected to it?" - *Yes*

"Why a UFO?" - *Experiment*

"On what?" - *Humans*

Is this why I saw the witches hat? Because ET tech is more like magic to humans?

"Is there still something there?" - *Yes…New Mexico*

"Underground?" - *Yes* - "What is it?"

I could see the image of a crystal in prism shape.

"Human accessible?" - *Maybe*

I could see a blue portal of energy. Swirling, like the color of the bluest sky. Then I could see a cliff again with the sedimentary lines. I got the sense that the ship was inside the cliff / Dead crew - Mummy

"Safe?" - *Yes*

I can see a guy with glasses and short hair. A second guy, older. Or is this the same guy but at a later date when he was decades older?

Now, I regret not asking why I was shown these guys. They were not military.

Rock wall - Scratches on the wall from tools - Digging (I can feel eyes watching me, again.)

Smokestack - Old cabin like from the mining days in the desert southwest - Nearby - Mining - Sluice from river

"Does military know of this location?" - *Yes*

"Can they access the location?" - *No*

<u>Blue portal</u> - *Only the right DNA can enter*

I see an ET face; it has a big head but not a Zeta gray being. Then I see an underground tunnel or mine shaft. Lastly, I see a chain or DNA.

I got two groups of numbers that could be map coordinates. They place the target just inside Arizona, but very near New Mexico.

Two separate times during this session, I could feel eyes or an entity watching me. Not sure if I have experienced this before with a crystal psychometry session. Now that I think about it, it was similar to how I have felt eyes on me when I've projected to the Sphinx, especially upon going into the underground chambers and tunnels below the Sphinx.

The crescent and triangle or boomerang symbol are interesting. If it wasn't my brain/subconscious adding it, then it is like the crescent and triangle symbols that I have seen in meditations on 4/4/23 specifically the symbols that the Mantis being showed me; tourmaline psychometry on 10/19/23; seen in my Akashic reading; and the insignia on the ET robes described by one of my psychic readings.

The idea that this UFO/Crystal/Portal is in New Mexico is also interesting. September 13, 2023, I did a Light Healing session with Bev. Lots of earth and grounding stuff came through, nothing E.T. But she said she got that I needed to "retrace your steps from a prior journey. Midwest to SW with big red rocks and plateaus. Something to do with

Lewis and Clark. Pyramids and Lapis Lazuli. I also feel like Gabby mentioned Sedona or SW area in a session, but I can't find it in my notes.

Strange that I got pseudo coordinates because I normally don't see numbers in meditations or psychometry sessions.

CHAPTER 52

NOT A BIGFOOT!

For months, I have felt an energy or presence on the back part of our property. We butt up against twelve acres of forest and I haven't been able to decipher if the entity is on our property or in the forest. So, I mentioned it to a psychic, and she said it felt like an ancient and lonely spirit. Suggested I try and make contact with it.

A few days later, I was outside working in the yard when I got the sense that energy was near again. I grabbed a bucket and walked uphill to the end of our property line. Staying on our side, I flipped the bucket over and took a seat.

During the year it is either cold, buggy, or hot, or a combination of these where we live. So, I don't ever meditate outside. But this time, I sat quietly and listened to the birds and the leaves rustle with the squirrels prepping for the winter.

I grounded myself. Set my chakra's spinning clockwise and went from root to crown. Then I spun up my heart chakra and envisioned that chakra coming out of my back and going up into the sky like a large antenna for broadcasting. I asked for help and guidance in this life from my Star Family. Whoever they may be. After some time, this popped in my head; "You are related to none; You are related to all."

Well, that is kind of a doozy. I'm either just an Earth soul reincarnating on Earth repeatedly or something more complex. Have I had so many lives on other planets that I'm kind of 'related to all'? Or is my Star Family an older, progenitor type race of beings? Multiple psychics have gotten the hit that a Star group I work with a lot is immortal. Or at least such a high density that they have surpassed death and incarnation.

Then again. Everything happens at once across all timelines. Time can rewind or go forward. Time is circular. Time is a sphere.

As my brain was melting down pondering the complexities of time; the out of place smell of honeysuckle wafted to me. That can't be. There isn't any of that anywhere near our home. And it was autumn, so all the flowers had finished blooming.

Then in my mind's eye, I saw a short being just to my right and behind a tree. It came out and stared at me.

"Baby Bigfoot?!" I said out loud. The little entity was about two feet tall and covered in hair. But sparse hair, not thick enough to really help as a winter coat. He had a little belt, and something slung over his shoulder.

"Puckwudgie!"

I'm not sure if I heard that with my ears or in my head.

"Oh my gosh, I'm so sorry. I did not mean to offend you." The little guy seemed annoyed but maybe not angry. "Hi, my name is Matt, and I live here with my family. We don't want any trouble, just wanted to introduce myself to my neighbor." The little guy just looked at me, didn't say anything. "We won't mess with any of your trees. We will stay on our side and if you could stay on your side, that would be great."

The Puckwudgie seemed mollified. It cocked its head to one side and focused on me with one inquisitive eye.

"Can I see you with my eyes someday?" I asked.

"Maybe."

Then the little guy walked behind a tree in my mind's eye and was gone. I'm still not sure if I heard his reply in my head or with my ears.

Since then, the presence I felt that day is usually absent. But it still shows up for a day or two before leaving again for a month or two.

A good practice that I recommend for people is to grid their home for protection. I have heard that as a person begins to wake up to consciousness and their psychic abilities, they become a bright light in the dark. It can attract lower frequency beings out of curiosity. I personally don't want any of these lower density beings messing with me or my family, especially my children when they sleep.

If you get five quartz crystals, you can use them to shield your property. You bury one at each corner of your property and then one in the center. As you bury each crystal, tell it you want it to protect your home and create a shield. Once the pieces are all buried, close your eyes and envision a crystal pyramid forming over your property. The four corners connect and then go up to a point above the center crystal. Crystal pyramid.

While burying the crystals around my property, I had the distinct feeling an entity was following me around. It would watch me bury the crystal and then after I walked away, it would investigate what I had done. I didn't get the sense it was the Puckwudgie during that time. Months later, Jennifer would have a healing session with Bev. Jennifer saw in her mind's eye that a Gnome with a red hat was living in our backyard at a wood debris pile. She got the sense the Gnome watched us and our kids when we were outside. It seemed friendly and looking back, I feel like that was probably the entity following me around while I set up the crystal grid for our home.

CHAPTER 53

MISSING 411

There is a strange phenomenon of missing people in the United States. Alaska is its own ball of wax. For a tiny population, an inordinate percentage of that population goes missing every year. I've seen estimates that over 20,000 people have gone missing in Alaska since the 1970s. Many of these missing person cases could be chalked up to the harsh weather and the many predators. There could and have been serial killers in the state. But many of the cases have a strange scenario surrounding them. For example, many people go missing while hiking the trails around large cities like Juneau, during good weather. Also, many planes go missing and no wreckage is ever found.

The lower 48 has its own set of many strange disappearances that are strangely centered around National Parks. Instances where a group of friends or a family will be walking on a trail together and suddenly someone in the group is missing and never found. Or a pair of hunters will stop, and one guy will go behind a tree to pee and come back to find his partner's hunting equipment lying on the ground and that person is never found again.

Lots of theories abound for what is happening to these people, from faking their death for insurance reasons or wanting a new life, to being snatched by a bear or mountain lion, to the extreme ideas like being grabbed by a Bigfoot or UFO or walking into a portal and not being able to return.

I'm going to share a crystal psychometry session where I saw what might be happening to some of these missing people.

I have a beautiful piece of quartz called an Elestial Quartz or Crocodile Quartz. It has many, many facets on it. Crystals seem to be natural supercomputers, energy devices, and storage devices. They power our electronics, make up our computer screens, and can store many gigabytes of data like a super thumb drive.

This session, I could not stop yawning as I was getting into it. When a lot of energy or spirit is coming in, I yawn, a lot. Different people have different quirks when the energy gets strong. One of my favorite Light Workers that I know has her stomach growl the entire time a session is going on. It is so funny!

In this crystal psychometry session, I tried my 'go up in frequency' method. I envisioned myself on a staircase in the middle of a void. I started at our native third density and as I walked up the stairs, I envisioned myself going up in density. When I reached the barrier between third and fourth density, there was a clear membrane that I pushed my way through. Then I'm at the next density level. I did this a couple of times and asked for my spirit family to come and communicate.

Nothing.

Eventually, I got frustrated. Left that staircase and sent my consciousness to Mount Shasta. I went to the southern merging area of Mount Shasta on the right and Mount Shastina on the left. Previously, I had seen the opening as a pile of rock rubble in this area with one of my other crystals. No matter how I tried to enter the mountain in that area, I failed every time.

While I pondered this, I suddenly found myself watching a young man in the forest. It looked just like the Mount Shasta area. I was on a river watching the kid play in his swim trunks and sandals. He was playing with his younger brother.

As I watched, I saw him happily plop down on a floating inter-tube toy. The river was only about knee deep, slow and wide. While he floated down the river, the little brother turned to get something from their picnic table. At that moment, I saw the older boy slip through a shimmery portal. It was clear see-through but had a shimmer.

The younger boy turned around to see the expansive river before him, his brother missing. He called out for his brother but there was no reply.

The older brother could see and hear his little brother, so he answered. Not hearing a response, the younger boy grew scared and ran into the woods. Likely back to their parents or campsite.

This greatly disturbed the older boy, and he stood up in the river. Grabbing his floaty, he sloshed his way through the river back to the bank. He jogged up the bank awkwardly in his sandals. Before he could get back to the picnic table with their food and toys, he slammed into an invisible barrier.

He appeared stunned. He tried to push past it with his hand. It was solid and invisible as far as he was concerned. He stood back and threw his inter-tube at the barrier. Without slowing, the floaty went through the invisible wall and bounced on the ground. I could see the shock on the boy's face. He grabbed his sandals and threw them one at a time. Both went through and landed near the inter-tube. Desperately, he took off his swim trunks and they passed through the barrier just as the other inanimate objects did. He hit the invisible barrier with a hammer fist. It just silently blocked his body.

At that moment, the younger brother and two adult men came scrambling down to the river. They paused at the picnic table before noticing the missing boy's toy and clothes on the riverbank. They ran and investigated the scattered remnants of the boy's life.

Sadly, I could see the lost boy slamming his hand against the invisible wall, over and over as he cried out for help.

Then the older brother disappeared. I watched the others scramble up and down the riverbank for a little before I slipped from that vision and back into my physical body, safely waiting in my home.

Sitting in my comfortable recliner, I felt empty and sad. Was that one of the things happening to people that go missing mysteriously in the woods? Is that why many times the Missing 411 type cases find the lost person's stuff but never the person?

How can a portal like that exist? Is it created by natural or unnatural causes?

If we consider that our planet Earth is hurtling through space at an estimated 66,600 mph, it seems like we could hit random anomalies in space. Like small wormholes or blackholes at any time or place on this planet.

CHAPTER 54

HAND CHAKRAS OR PORTALS?

IN A SESSION WITH GABBY.

A very high density being came through with a message. I told her to only do what she felt comfortable with. She decided it was okay and went on to channel the Time Weaver for 8 minutes and 6 seconds. At this point I had worked with Gabby probably a dozen times. It was incredible to see her mannerisms change. Breathing and voice. During the channeling, Gabby was constantly using one or both hands to emphasize what was being relayed. Gabby never talks with her hands, not before or since this channeling.

I think the message was meant to relieve my anxiety about who my Star Family might be. I don't know if I felt better, but it did give me some clarification about that and how time works. Most of the message was about how time is circular, cyclical, and can be moved forward or backwards depending on the need. The entity also pointed out that the numbers 3, 6, and 9 were very important in the universe. Her channeling was 8 minutes and 6 seconds long. Three, 6, and 9 would become important again in the near future. Nikola Tesla was also obsessed with 3, 6, and 9 and said it was the keys to the universe.

Within an hour of finishing that session with Gabby, a weird energy built up in my hands. It was like warm electricity. You know when you fall on pavement and catch yourself with your hands? That low burning and pressure feeling from catching your weight and the slight abrasions against your skin. That is what my hands felt like.

That feeling lasted for nine days straight. Yeah, 9 again. How do you even make this up?

On day ten, the feeling had decreased greatly and after that it became intermittent. My hands would feel normal for a few hours and then light up again for a few hours. Over the next couple of weeks this would continue until the sensations were there but much more subtle. Interestingly, by that time the energy was mostly only present in my left hand with my right hand being about one-third the intensity of my left.

Being the scientist and skeptic, I was trained to be, I started pinging my network of psychics to see if I could get some insight and collaboration among them.

What the hand energy was fell into two schools of thought: (1) hand chakra activation, (2) portals in my hands.

From there, opinions as to what it was for varied. Some got hits that it was for healing. One thought I was unconsciously using the energy to help activate other people around me. And another thought my left receiving hand is pulling in energy that I'm to take to other places and expel through my right giving hand. The most interesting to me was the hit one practitioner got that it was Arcturians working with me. She laughed and said they were trying to increase the activity of my third eye and the energy was spilling out my left hand. They told her that they make mistakes with the human body sometimes!

I don't think one is more 'right' over any other. Heck, I'm learning that it is just as easily everything than it is nothing. And all of those actually resonate with me based on my experiences in past psychic readings and my own meditations.

Let's examine the Arcturian angle. The blue-gray skinned beings known as Arcturians are from the area near Arcturus, the Alpha star in the Bootes constellation. They are believed to be a benevolent race of ancient beings. More alien in appearance than say the Nordic types of beings from the Pleiades star system.

It is believed by some that there is a shorter version of Arcturians and a giant-sized version from a different planet. Keep in mind that, just like our star system, there could be multiple planets in a single star system that supports life and advanced civilizations. It would make sense that if a group of sentient beings colonized another planet, the colonizers would adapt to the differences on that planet and eventually look quite different than the sister beings on the home planet. Given enough evolutionary time, of course. It could be caused by differences between the planets in gravity, day length, season length, atmospheric differences in gases, and habitat differences.

Let's throw out the idea that I'm batshit crazy and roll with this.

Looking through my notes, there are many mentions of Arcturians or Arcturian energy coming through that my psychics picked up on over the years. In one of my meditations, I was image streaming and the last thing I got after some ET stuff was 'Bootes'. At the time I didn't know what it was. I was shocked to see that when I looked it up it was a star constellation that contained the Arcturus star. Then later while Cairo, Egypt, the first night there I looked up at the stars and the first I noticed was a large orange star. My star chart app on my phone confirmed that it was the star Arcturus.

Another interaction with my QHHT practitioner in a small group session. It was the first time I had gone out in 'community' to do something Woo. Sure, I love taking my family to the gem and fossil show that is full of Woo-Woo people, but you can respectfully attend that without worrying about your coworkers or clients thinking you are a nut job.

Anyways, that session Bev was leading an Ancestral Contracts Clearing workshop. The focus was connecting to your family lineage and then cutting any contracts that no longer have a use. It was very Native American in flavor. In the beginning, in my mind's eye I saw myself and my ancestral line as black wolves after the suggestion from Bev's process. We were running through the woods. But at some point, I morphed into a black and red-colored dragon. My wolf pack morphed into different colored dragons. When Bev got to where I was laying on the floor with my feet facing her, she grasped my socked feet and repeated what she saw.

"Arcturians are present. You are loved and honored beyond measure. Activation of the Crown and 3rd Eye." Later, afterwards she expounded and said she saw three Arcturians call me 'Commander' and they placed a new emblem on my chest signifying a new rank. But what was strange, was after she let go of my feet and moved on to the next person, I could still feel someone holding my feet! With my eyes closed, I only knew Bev had moved on because I heard her voice change position. The idea that the Arcturians were holding my feet nearly made me jump up, interrupt the whole session, and run out into the street!

Now, Bev knows nothing of me and Arcturians. They didn't come up in my QHHT session and I haven't mentioned any of my other run-ins with them to her. Even if she were to make it up in the moment, it is way more likely she would say the Pleiadeans were there. Pleiadeans are kind of the 'go to' ET species for the last couple of decades in UFO circles. Being the most human-like in appearance seems to help Earthlings resonate with them over say, a Mantid or Zeta Gray ET.

Bev also didn't know, that in a session to specifically try and figure out what ET lives I might have lived in a past life regression, I saw myself as one of the tall Arcturians. In the one Akashic Records reading I've had; I was also informed that I was a 'Blue Ray'. This term means that I had many lives on many planets, including at least two lives in Arcturus. And specifically, in one of those lives, I was twelve feet tall and commanded many ships and fleets. That sounds an awful lot like Bev's Arcturians calling me Commander. It also reminds me of the meditation I did where I was in an ET body floating in space and I came into that ship with all the soldiers saluting me!

I wish I had a head-exploding emoji to put here!

What about the idea that my hands are for collecting some kind of Earth energy to move it around?

Maybe not as fantastical as ETs, but there might be something to this. I love crystals and attend gem shows and search out crystal shops when I travel with my kids for their hockey games and tournaments around the east coast. Since the energy appeared in my hands, I can sometimes find crystals in these stores that cause my left hand to flare up when I hover it over the stone. My 10-year-old son is proving better at it than I am.

I have always been a little claustrophobic. But after my hands activated, for lack of a better term. I've started encountering these cave tourist attractions. The last two tournaments we went to, one with my son in New York State and one with my daughter in Pennsylvania, we have stumbled upon these cave tours. Without consciously seeking them out, one was on the drive to the venue and the other was five minutes from our hotel. Ignoring my claustrophobia, I felt compelled to visit both and we did.

Outside both caves, while waiting in the parking lots for our tour time, my left hand started to power up and go from nothing to intense. Once down in the caves, the intensity of the energy in my hand ebbed and flowed. And despite my usual claustrophobia, I felt completely at peace through the entire tour at both locations.

I don't know. Could be any of those or all of those. But like I mentioned before, I think most of the stuff that people encounter in the Wooniverse is never black and white and a single thing. It is truly many things.

CHAPTER 55

THE RETURN OF MY WIFE

IT WAS A BRUTAL FIVE MONTHS OF CHEMOTHERAPY FOR JENNIFER, THE KIDS, AND THE DOGS.

During all that, we had puppies. But before our dog gave birth, I was dozing on the bed one afternoon when she jumped up with me and eased herself down. I stirred just enough to put my hand on her ribs and started to doze off again. Before I could, I saw my dog from childhood, Ginger. She was such a great dog. Super smart but her life was cut short by a delivery truck.

Next, in my mind's eye I saw Ginger running. She turned into a rainbow of colors and jumped into the body of our pregnant dog!

I shot up in the bed and started crying. I loved Ginger so much and now I knew that she had come back to me. She was going to reincarnate in one of these puppies!

I started to get nervous that I wouldn't know which puppy was Ginger. Turns out, when the puppies were born, I knew instantly which one was Ginger's reincarnation. It was the only puppy with the blonde brindle coat that I had wanted for so many years now. And it was a boy, which was totally against my wife's desire to keep a girl. Needless to say, he's a part of the family now. I wasn't losing that battle.

Our kids loved the puppies, but then the travel hockey season got going and not having a second parent to help beat me down. Normally, I helped coach both kid's teams and split the games on the weekends with Jennifer. That meant I was at an ice rink seven days a week. Jennifer's assistance was a no go this season, but somehow, I managed to get the kids to all four games over most weekends. Tournaments were tough without help. Those are long three- or four-day weekends anywhere from two to six hours from home. So, the kid that didn't have the tournament had to miss their games on those weekends. Tough on my son because he was the youngest on his team and between that and coaching through nepotism, his head coach made sure my son didn't play much. My daughter is a goalie but luckily her team had a backup goalie, so it wasn't as detrimental for her to miss a game as it was for my son.

School was tough for our youngest without her mom. I had managed to avoid attending most school things over the last six years because of work obligations, so our daughter wasn't in love with dad helping out at school. It was funny and exhausting at the same time. But we all survived.

Then, even though Jennifer still had three more surgeries to deal with, she finally came out of the chemo fog. Her appetite returned and she started physical therapy. Little steps. Her helping drive the kids to school or pick them up after school was a magical relief for me. I honestly don't know how single parents manage and they have all my respect after this time in my life.

"What are you smiling about," Jennifer asked me.

"Nothing," I grinned. She gave me her annoyed side-eye look. "I'm just glad to have my wife back."

She snorted derisively. "I didn't go anywhere and I'm far from 'back'. What are you really smiling about?"

"Really, I'm glad to have you up and a little more active again."

"And?"

"And I'm beyond excited to be going to that past life regression retreat in Jupiter, Florida next week. For months, I've felt like there is someone important there that I'm supposed to meet."

"I want to go to Florida. I'm tired of winter." Jennifer complained. "But I am glad you are finally going to find your 'community'," she chuckled. She was referring to me telling her how all these different psychics kept telling me that spirit wants me to go out and find community.

"Me too! Me too. Bring on the weirdos, my people!"

CHAPTER 56

JUPITER

One funny thing about this Florida retreat, was the fact that before I booked it, I purchased a rock that looks like the planet Jupiter. It is a polished piece of jasper; red, pink, orange, brown, gray, and white. The whole stone is a swirl of colors like Jupiter. But it gets better. The whole stone is shades of red, brown, orange, pink, white and then on one side is a large gray spot surrounded by an orange line, surrounded by a brown line, surrounded by red. It resembles the planet Jupiter with its perpetual storm spot so much that it is uncanny.

Before the trip to Jupiter, I did a psychometry session with this stone. I got a fascinating string of animals that all have status as protectors or good luck in various cultures.

Initially, I saw a dog but then it morphed into a jackal and then Anubis. Then the image streaming just flowed.

Snake - Japanese Lion (*known as Komainu or gate protector*) - Swan - Bat - Fish - Dragon - Lotus flower - and finally I heard the words "Spiritual Protector".

This trip to Florida was my first non-working vacation in the ten years since I started my company. So, I flew in early the day before to take full advantage of my time. It was an hour from the airport to my hotel near the beach. I wasted no time checking in, changing into shorts, and hitting the beach. The weekend before I had been in Lake Placid with my son's hockey team, and it had been 3 degrees Fahrenheit. So, this chance to walk the beach shirtless and shoeless was heaven sent.

There was a little cloud cover and a steady breeze. I just started walking. My path drifted in and out of the waves. I quickly went from my root chakra to my crown, activating each chakra and then I just focused on grounding myself. The sand wasn't as nice as the California beaches of my youth, but it was a lot nicer than the large coarse sand of New Jersey.

I just walked and walked. Before I knew it, two hours had passed and according to my watch, I had far surpassed my step's goal for the day.

As I was beginning to think about what I would do for dinner, my watch alerted me to a text. The day before this trip, I crawled out of my independent shell and asked the Jupiter group if I could join the carpool group that had formed at the hotel I was staying at. I have never done that in the past. Normally, I would do everything on my own and avoid people.

According to the text, some of the carpool group had arrived early and planned to go to dinner. Again, normally I would just go solo all night. But I felt compelled to hop in the group chat and count myself in. Besides, they were going to a fish restaurant and where else do you eat when you visit Florida?

We arrived at the restaurant and went through introductions. There was Crystal and her sister Daisy. They reminded me of my brother and I, where if you looked hard you could say they looked related. Only these sisters seemed to be on good terms and my brother, and I have always been on so-so terms. Then Claire was the only dark-haired woman in the group, and she had a great smile. She seemed like someone that talked to people for her work. Finally, was Dawn, she had a big energy and laugh. She reminded me of my wife. I would later learn they both had infectious laughs and a penchant for quick online searches of restaurants when we needed one.

I was told we were missing one person, Bob. His flight was later in the evening so we wouldn't see him until the morning when we got together to carpool to the retreat location. So, in total we were a group of six. Yep, that number again.

Dinner was genuinely fun. We were complete strangers, and yet we had so much stuff to talk about. I guess it's because none of us had friends that dabbled in the Wooniverse, so finally having like-minded people to talk to was incredible. Much against my normal attitude, I didn't want this dinner to end.

I felt an instant connection to everyone at the table. I was sitting next to Crystal and oddly, after two minutes of being around her, I was ready to tell her my life story. It was completely out of the ordinary for me and how I had lived my life for the last forty-seven years.

CHAPTER 57

THE CABIN IN THE WOODS

JANUARY 26, 2024

The next morning, our group of six was so eager to get to the retreat location, that we left plenty early. From the beach, we drove directly inland for about twenty minutes. There had been some construction near our hotel, so we were worried that being a Friday morning, we would get delayed and none of us wanted to be late.

Once we got off the highway we meandered through neighborhoods with large lots and there were many coniferous trees. It is not the kind of habitat most visitors to Florida expect.

Eventually, we made it to the house that we would be conducting QHHT past life regressions, meditations, and other modalities. My jaw almost hit my lap when we pulled into the driveway. The house was an older log cabin. A log cabin in Florida!

My marveling at the cabin would be short-lived. We hopped out of the SUV we shared and then the nervous introductions began. I hate these. We were all there for the same thing. We all had been following either the career of Savannah or the other host, Samantha. I had seen Samantha on shows in passing, but her body of work was new to me. She was also a QHHT practitioner, but I didn't realize she was like royalty in that space. There were a lot of retreat attendees that were newer QHHT practitioners, and they were quick to let me know of my ignorance.

I was pleasantly surprised to see that out of almost forty attendees, there were nearly as many men as women. Being my first event like this, I didn't know what to expect, but I figured it would be mostly women. After all, that one ancestral healing session that I had done a few weeks earlier had been me and seven other women.

Eventually, everyone had a name tag and a new journal. We were ushered inside, and everyone found a seat with Samantha and Savannah centrally located next to the fireplace and facing the group crammed into the living room.

Our guides for the weekend went through introducing themselves, and then all the attendees took turns introducing themselves. The energy in the room was bombastic. Normally, I would have put up my energy shield before walking into a place like this. But I just felt it was important to let the energy flow. If it became too much, I could always throw up my shield and slowly recuperate over the next hour or two.

The group of collected souls were so interesting. There were women of every age, and the guys ranged from military pilot to real estate broker, to bee shaman. It was so fun to finally be out of my Woo closet!

We went through some discussions about the schedule for the weekend and then jumped right into an 'easy' regression. The first one, we just traveled to ourselves as children when we were happy. I saw myself in my late teens, snowboarding. I heard in my head, "remember to have fun". That was the easiest it was going to be for the weekend as we were all going to see very quickly.

The next was a full-on deep past life regression. Savannah led the room through a deep hypnosis until we were walking down a hallway. Mine was a stone tunnel, like in a castle. The tunnel was lined with different colored doors on either side. They appeared to be wooden doors with big wrought iron handles.

Walking down the hallway, I stopped at a yellow door. Savannah gave us the prompt to open the door and go inside.

The vision in my mind's eye slowly took form. It was a man. He slowly came into focus.

"Oh, shit! I'm fucking Hitler!" I screamed in my head.

No, wait, I'm looking at Hitler. I quickly looked down at my feet. Black shiny shoes. Green uniform. I have a lot of military medals on my breast. I'm older, early fifties.

Shit, I'm a general in Hitler's inner circle. We are in a meeting with him. There is no more than a dozen of us.

Savannah prompted us to move forward in time to where we live.

I'm standing in front of a two-story row house. It is very European. Cobblestone street and many homes lined up like a row sharing walls. This home is big and nice. I'm inside now, sitting at the dinner table. I can see my blonde wife. I have a son and two younger daughters. The girls are twins. We all have blonde or light brown hair. We are laughing.

Savannah prodded us to move forward to an important day in this life.

Bombing!

Bombs are dropping everywhere. I'm underground. Each bomb shakes us and dirt falls from the ceiling. The lights flicker with each earth shake.

Suddenly, I'm somewhere else. It is green and tropical, and I get the feeling it is Venezuela. I'm living on a sugar cane farm.

Savannah brought us to the end of our lives.

I'm an old man. I'm lying in my bed at the end of my life. Alone. I'm staring out the window at the tropical forest around me. I'm full of guilt for being on the wrong side of history. My family is gone. I feel guilty for surviving when so many didn't.

Savannah pulled us out of our hypnosis. "Now, don't say anything. Grab your journals and spread out, go outside, find a spot and just write what happened."

The room was somber. I guess I wasn't the only one that had something heavy. I headed outside and made a straight line for the fire pit because it had Adirondack chairs. Strangely, those chairs don't hurt my back.

After I scribbled down what happened, I closed my eyes and just sat with it. Let the thoughts come through.

I have not always been on the side of light. I had much guilt in that life for living to an old age. But I don't need that guilt anymore. It no longer serves me in this life. I can't control everything around me. I need to let my kids deal with their own stuff, even though I hate my son's hockey coach.

The Universe is dichotomy. Takes Darkness for there to be Light.

That humbling past life aside, the group moved on to Samantha's modality for pendulum dowsing. Everyone was given a rose quartz pendulum and a sheet of paper with a circular wheel encompassed by the alphabet. Apparently, the rose quartz material is important because of the high love energy in the pink stone. I totally get it.

We were talked through Samantha's methodology and some folks were amazed with how easily that modality came to them. My pendulum was anemic, and I just had this deep feeling it wasn't for me. Like maybe it is too slow, and I shouldn't waste my time learning it? I don't know, that was just the feeling that I got over the weekend. Well, that, and the pendulum kept falling off its chain. No one else seemed to have that problem, so maybe my difficulties were a message from the Wooniverse?

We wrapped up the first day with an activity called Eye Gazing. This was new for most of us, including me. The simple part of it is, the group splits in two and faces each other. Luckily, we had an even number of people with Samantha the odd woman out so she could track the timer. Then each person stepped right up to each other, and I mean right up to each other. The job was to stare in each other's eyes for one minute.

That is not as easy as it sounds. In our culture, we look away when we speak to each other. Our eyes are the windows to our souls. So, it takes a lot of trust to allow another person to stare into your eyes for a minute without looking away. I quickly grounded myself and ran up my chakras getting them spinning and flowing.

We got going and it was a little uncomfortable. At first, you try to decide if you look at their right eye or left eye. Or does it make more sense to go back and forth between the eyes? Eventually, I settled on picking one eye and locking into it for the entire minute. I could feel what I've come to believe is Arcturian energy that comes in behind me. I felt a giant Arcturian being standing behind me. Then I psychically felt up and connected to Source to pull down energy into my crown chakra. I pulled Earth energy up from my feet. And I felt orange energy coming in through my back from the Arcturian entity behind me. All three energies coalesced in my heart chakra. During the gazing, I imagined myself sending orange energy to the other persons heart chakra. I also repeated the mantra, 'thank you for being you, thank you for being here', inside my head.

After a few participants passed, I began to hear words in my head. I don't know if it was my Higher Self or the unseen entity behind me, but the first time it happened I was looking into the dark brown eyes of a gentleman and in my had I heard, 'Zeta'.

Whoa. This guy came from a Zeta star family. A couple people later it happened again with another man with dark eyes.

Then, with one guy, while watching his eye, I saw a slit form down from the pupil. It stayed until the minute was up and I heard 'Reptilian' in my head. It makes sense, you can be from any star family. Heck, some people could have had lives on many planets and maybe this gentleman had a life as a Reptilian somewhere. I mean, in a meditation in Lake Placid, my consciousness drifted into the mountain to what seemed to be abandoned tunnels. I saw some kind of natural Earth Reptoid species that had lived there at one time long ago.

There was one woman in the group that seemed very mature for her young age. When she took up place before me, her deep brown eyes felt like a kindred spirit to me. As I watched her serene eyes, my two Feline-human bodyguards that had been standing behind me walked over and stood on either side of her. Ah, she must have some Feline star lineage in her, I thought. There actions were as blatant as hearing it in my head.

Another guy that seemed like the big jolly man of the group got close to me in the line. I liked him. His name was Jeff. He reached out and patted me on the shoulder, "It's you and me next buddy!"

I was kind of groggy from the whole thing, so I just nodded. I couldn't even get out any words before I gazed into the eyes of the woman in front of me. Nothing much happened and then it was time for me and the jolly man. We got started and he was grinning. I grinned back and then got serious again. Jeff seemed to take my lead as he suddenly stiffened and his smile drooped into a stern slit. I didn't hear anything in my head and my spirit guards stayed put behind me. But and I mean but, his eyes slowly changed from light brown to gray. Literally gray eyes! It was amazing.

No matter how hard I focused, I couldn't get a feel for why it was happening, and I didn't hear any voices in my head. Samantha ended that session and Jeff almost stumbled. He mumbled something and moved down the line.

I reached the end of the line. Two women left to go. Both were blonde with light blue eyes and had come separately. When I started with the first of the two, I heard a loud 'Taygetan' in my head. That startled me, but not to be outdone was my spirit dragon. He had been lying on the roof of the cabin all day. But during the gaze with this woman, Ragnar lowered his massive head and came up behind her to check her out. I was stunned. Nearly twenty people into this gazing ceremony and he hadn't taken any interest in it until this woman!

On to the last person. The other blonde. I got the same Pleiades feel from her. Taygeta is a star in the Pleiades, so I could easily see how both women came from a Pleiades star family. Then, Ragnar lowered his head and looked at the back of this woman too! What the heck! They must be connected somehow.

"Okay, that is time," Samantha said. "How does everyone feel?" The crowd, so boisterous at the beginning was now subdued. Some folks blinked; others muttered. "Well, could you tell that we moved from one minute to two minutes during the sessions?"

Everyone broke into chattering. That got us going. We were stunned to learn we had been peering into the eyes of another person for two whole minutes!

As we broke up to go inside and gather our things, I grabbed the two blondes. "I saw something interesting if you would like me to share, but I don't have to."

The younger woman, blinked in surprise. "Yes, of course. Please tell me." The other blonde nodded and stepped up.

"Well, I sound like an idiot, but I have a dragon in my spirit team."

"What! What does he look like?" Asked the younger woman excitedly.

"Well, he's black and huge." I looked up at the roof of the cabin. "He's been hanging out up there all day. He has seemed disinterested in everything until I got to the gazing with both of you." I was shocked to see neither woman seemed skeptical but genuinely interested. "When I got to you, I heard "Taygetan" in my head and my dragon came down and looked at you. Then when I got to you," I turned to the older woman, "I got the same Pleiadian vibe, and my dragon came down again and looked at you too."

The older woman stepped in closer. "What is Taygetan or Pleiadian?"

"Have you heard of the Nordic ETs?" I asked. The younger woman nodded. "People think those beings that look just like humans are from the Pleiades star cluster and one of the seven stars there is Taygeta." I suddenly wondered if I had just branded myself a nutter for the rest of the weekend.

"Wow. Thank you so much for sharing." The younger woman said genuinely. I would later learn she had strong medium abilities to speak with passed on family members. The other nodded her head and we all made our way inside.

CHAPTER 58

ORION WARS

JANUARY 27, 2024

The next morning, I woke invigorated. It was shocking considering how crowds usually take their toll on me. Another strike against me should have been my terrible hotel mattress that was slanted at an angle, so there was no comfy position. Regardless, I was up early so I drove to the beach to watch the sunrise. Wispy clouds dotted the horizon that morning and the sunrise was a glorious collage of yellows, reds, oranges, and pinks. I grew up on the West Coast where this would have been a sunset. East Coast sunrises always strike me as odd.

Next, it was more delicious coffee from the nearby coffee/ice cream shack and back to the hotel to meet my carpool group. They were easily like family after an arguably short time together. I could effortlessly talk to any of the five and not run out of things to say.

We traveled to the cabin together and quickly jumped into our first past life regression session.

I found myself walking down the same set of stone stairs as the day before as Savannah dropped us into a hypnotic state. I shuffled down the same stone tunnel lined with colorful doors on both sides. This time I found myself stopping before a purple door. Like the day before, I opened the door and stepped through.

It was daytime. I gazed across a pastoral scene of rolling hills with an alien city in the distance. I could see people, no, beings working the fields. Looked like large vegetable gardens more than today's row crops.

I gazed down at my feet and up my body to see if I was non-human like the workers in the fields. I had three toes and three fingers. My body was skinny and lanky. I was very tall. My arms and legs were disproportionally long. My skin was a base gray with darker gray lines spidering out making a mottled web of lines over the lighter gray color.

The city in the distance was completely unique. It consisted of buildings reminiscent of champagne glasses placed upside down. The homes, I assumed they were homes, were a cylinder up for a couple of stories and then they narrowed rapidly and extended up another two stories like a spike, or radio tower of some kind. The exteriors shimmered gold, bronze, and copper colors like they had a metal veneer. They glinted magnificently in the late day sun.

Feeling into this life, I could tell I was normally a farmer. Most everyone in this society farmed food.

Unexpectedly, strange flying ships flew over the landscape firing lasers at us! People scattered everywhere seeking shelter. I ran at full speed down my lookout hill and across the fields. I felt I had to reach the city. I had to find my family and protect them.

Savannah prompted the group to move forward to an important day in this life.

I saw myself fighting the invaders. I had some kind of arm cannon weapon. The opening at the end had layers like an unopened rose bud. It slipped over my forearm and discharged a plasma type round. Not lasers but more like molten lava.

Unfortunately, we were not a warrior race. The invaders were parasites conquering planets and stripping them of resources. I got the sense this was during the Orion Wars.

Draco Reptilians. Invaders. Parasites. Scourge.

I hate them. They used us as slaves to mine our own planet. They beat me and the other slaves to make us work harder. My people were regularly beaten to death while on the job.

The last day of this life was brutal. I was strung up spread eagle. My legs were tied down. It was pulling my shoulder joints, my vertebrae, my hips and knees. The pain burned in my joints.

I can see a Draco Reptilian beating me. He grows board with it and picks up an odd-looking sword from a table cluttered with torture implements.

This is it. This disgusting Invader sliced me in half below my ribcage.

With my death, I returned to Source. I've been here before. Source shares with me that I have had many lives across the galaxy over eons. This life's lesson was to break the Reptilian control and ascend. Accept what they did and move on.

Weeks after this, I did an Akashic Reading with a practitioner that specialized in Galactic Records. One section of my reading seems to be hitting on this life.

"Andromedins are bringing up Reptilian energy," the Akashic reader shifted gears. "And it's not to fear any particular people. It is just to share that there were some experiences where…how are they sharing this? Basically, I'm being shown you as a being, and you are getting dragged is the best way I can describe it. And almost being forced to do things that you don't want to do and it feels like being very powerless. So even though there were lots of beautiful lifetimes and memories, this is one that kind of stood out and that is being cleared up."

CHAPTER 59

AUTOMATIC WRITING AND ATLANTIS

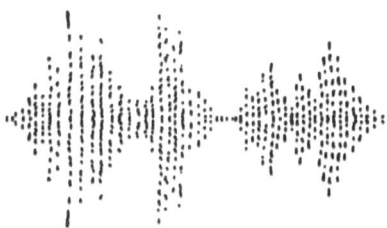

Early the next morning, I sort of woke up and absorbed the dream I just exited. Then I fell back to sleep.

A few hours later, I woke and quickly went to get a cup of coffee. Before driving back to the hotel, I rolled the dream over in my head.

I think I saw Lumeria, or maybe Atlantis.

I was in a large temple. Not like any church of the 20th Century but more natural or rustic. No one wore shoes and the floor was dirt. Not because it was primitive, but because the soles of shoes block us from the Earth energy. Today's rubber-soled shoes are especially good insulators that stop us from connecting and grounding. This stops the energy from flowing into our feet. It breaks the circuit between our bodies and the Earth.

There was a massive crocodile quartz crystal in the center of the temple. It was probably the size of a school bus standing on end. It had a beautiful rainbow sheen that rippled along the side as the viewer moved.

A blonde woman with a large crystal tiara seemed to be the Priestess. People came here to be healed by her and the crystal. Everyone used to be able to do this on their own, but we had forgotten and now the Priestess facilitates it for the populace. She wore a white gown, and her many acolytes wore peach-colored gowns. The acolytes lacked any ornamentation like the Priestess' necklace and tiara.

That seemed to be the gist of it. I got my delicious coffee and walked back to my rental car. As I sat in the seat some knowing suddenly hit me with force. I could almost feel it in my guts. There was another message under the dream. Like when you look at video editing software. There is the video stream and below that is the audio feed graphic. There was an audio feed to that dream that was in me and needed to get out.

I raced back to the hotel and almost sprinted to my room. Grabbing my journal I just started writing what came to mind and didn't question it.

By coming together the group energy is amplified by a high level. Without knowing it, many attendees are activating those around them. Most powerful activations happening between those of shared star families.

All information and knowing is available to every entity. Doubts and fears must be dropped to enable access to the universal network of knowing.

Some here have the knowledge they seek just beyond their fingernails; some are touching with their fingertips, and few have their fingers in the pot.

With practice and energy everyone can reach their hands in the candy bowl.

Whoa…That was automatic writing. I have been told so many times by so many people of the Woo that I should be able to do it. But this is the first time it has happened, and it was powerful. It felt like another being was whispering in my ear and I just wrote down what I heard. For example, "reach their hands in the candy bowl." Who says that? I would have said the cookie jar.

My past life regression that afternoon fit a running theme that I am beginning to unravel.

I went through my door into another pastoral world. This was very medieval. I was a middle-aged man. My arms were hairy, and my clothes were simple. I had a rucksack and a golden necklace with a red gem. It was course jewelry, far from ornate. I could sense that I was a hunter by trade. I had a wife but we were unable to have children. This felt like Earth.

I exited the woods with a deer slung over my shoulder. I gazed across a valley with farmlands and short rock walls dividing up plots. Near the middle of the valley was a small village. The homes were simple squares with stacked stones making the first couple of feet from the ground and then what looked like clay creating the rest of the wall up to the thatch roofs. The mountains in the distance were very odd. They were so jagged along the summits that it seemed more like a child's painting, very surreal.

Savannah prompted the group to move forward to an important day. I didn't want to see this. My wife was hanging from gallows in the middle of town. She was dead. The town had killed her while I was gone one day. I don't know why, but I feel like it was related to religion.

Next, I saw a tombstone, but strangely it was made of wood.

I lived many more years in this life. Lonely, quiet years. Prodded to see the end of this life by Savannah, I saw myself gray haired and heavily bearded. I was fighting a bear and losing. It didn't take long for the bear to overpower me and end my life.

The lesson of that life was to appreciate and cherish my wife and kids in this current life. My Higher Self came through stronger than it usually does in these regressions.

Be Happy. Do what makes you happiest. Find someone to take over your business.

I saw a large pyramid that was made up of smaller stacked pyramids. It reminded me of my son's Rubik's cube that was in the shape of a pyramid.

Accept all your gifts to clear your eyes.

Well, that is interesting. I've always wanted to try to heal my astigmatism with QHHT.

A few days later, driving to the airport, I passed two buildings with glass pyramids on top. Each pyramid was a framework of smaller pyramids and gold in color. It looked exactly like the pyramid I saw at the end of the hunter life!

CHAPTER 60

DRAGON CLAN 6

Later, my group and I were eating dinner. I brought up the idea that had struck me earlier that day when entering my hotel room.

"You know, there are six of us. Three, six, nine, they are power numbers in the universe. Tesla believed that and it makes sense to me." I can be long winded at times. "So, my hotel room number is 123. One plus two is three plus three is six. What are your guys' room numbers."

We were all amazed to calculate out that everyone's room could be added, subtracted, or multiplied to get to six just like the number in our group. All except Crystal and Daisy, the two sisters.

"Ah, it doesn't work for us," Daisy said, a little disappointed.

"Well, now wait a minute," Bob interjected. "You are sisters, what if you combine both your room numbers."

"Yeah, totally!" Cheered Dawn.

I scribbled on the paper that I had been using. "It totally works, if you use the numbers from both their rooms you get to six!" I said excitedly.

"You are two sides of the same coin," Dawn said.

Maybe it means nothing, but it seemed profound to us at the time.

"Okay, now birthdays," I said.

"Ooh, yeah, birthdays," Claire egged us on.

We worked through everyone's birthdays. Some of us could get to six with our birth year. Some with our birth month and day. And the last in the group took some work, but we even managed to get six with her birth month, day, and year.

"Synchronicity," Crystal smiled.

We all pondered the idea that somehow the Universe brought all six of us together to this weekend retreat. Got all of us to stay at the same hotel. Got us into a carpool group that went to dinner together every night over the long weekend. Our hotel rooms and birthdays could also be broken down into the number six. Surely it can't all be coincidence.

"Dragon Clan 6," I said. Everyone looked at me. "That is what this group is."

CHAPTER 61

SAYING GOODBYES

JANUARY 29, 2024

On the last day, I found myself alone in the kitchen with Samantha. Somehow, we got onto the topic of Egypt, and I shared the three meditations where I traveled to the Sphinx before the pyramids were built. When I told her about what I saw under the Sphinx her eyes widened.

"Have you been to Egypt?"

"No," I answered. "But I know I need to go there. Every time I meditate, I see pyramids. And, I have Khufu and Imhotep as spirit guides, so I'm supposed to go there. Plus, I saw myself as a female Sirian at the time of the pyramids. Saw the pyramids being built by men and giants."

"Oh my god. You have to go. Savannah and I have a trip in May."

"I know, I saw that it was full."

"Okay," Savannah started. "May in Egypt is magical. That tour is full but if you want to go, I'll make room for you."

Now it was my turn for my eyes to bulge. "Of course I want to go. But it is a matter of if my wife will let me go. It's a big deal and expensive and she has surgeries to do this year."

"Totally understand. But we sort of had a spot that we were keeping or going to just let go, I'll hold that spot for you. Just let me know if you can pull it off."

I was beaming. I hadn't smiled that hard all weekend and I had spent the entire weekend smiling from ear to ear. But to be honest, I have no idea how to convince my wife to let me leave the country for two weeks and spend that much money.

It had been three long days of spiritual growth and inner work. Some Dark Night of the Soul work for many. We were invigorated and tired at the same time as we said our goodbyes to the group, our amazing hosts, and the land that had sheltered us.

Dragon Clan 6 decided to eat dinner together one last time. Half of us were staying at the hotel one more night and the rest were driving home after dinner. Nothing sorrowful about saying goodbye. We were just as jazzed as we had been on the first night together.

We all felt like we had our Tribe now and looked forward to continuing our group communications moving forward.

I must admit, with all my nerve and sciatic pain from three herniated discs and surgeries, I was really worried that the plane ride to Florida would have me in pain for the whole weekend. Then, with as lovely as the cabin in the woods where we all met was for our sessions, it was full of plastic chairs and uncomfortable couches. Again, I was positive they were going to kill my back. But somehow, as I got on that plane ride home, I hadn't had a single spasm of back pain the entire extended weekend. Despite my hotel mattress being one of the worst I've ever slept in!

I have hated flying since forever. With my bad anxiety, I had reached a point of taking a Xanax before every flight. However, I didn't take one to fly down or fly back from Florida. So, an hour into the flight home, it was odd when I got anxious.

I had the sudden thought that I should write my book. That book I had started nine (yes, nine) months earlier. I often felt like I needed to write it, like spirit was pushing me in that direction.

I pulled out my iPad and opened the book writing app. I had only written one chapter. I remember the day I did it, I was sitting on the front porch, three bourbons on ice (yeah, three again) into my evening when I wrote a single chapter. Then for some reason, I set it aside and didn't look at it or work on it again for the last nine months.

That's it, I'm going to work on this again, I thought to myself. I didn't want to work on it now with all these strangers around me, so I closed the iPad and put it back in my bag at my feet. Within a minute I got hit with brutal anxiety. My chest was tight, and it was hard to breathe.

What the heck, we are already in the air and far from landing. I need to sit with this anxiety and find out why I have it.

I closed my eyes and concentrated. The book. I need to write it, or Spirit isn't going to leave me alone.

Okay, I thought. I get it guys. I will write it, but I don't want to work on it now.

Instantly, the anxiety relaxed. It did not return the rest of the flight or even that day.

It has been a fun, fascinating, and frustrating last three years post pandemic. My spiritual awakening is well on its way despite 3D life muddying the waters along the way.

I want to share one last thing I was told in my Akashic Reading that I believe pertains to writing this book.

An academic side to all this. You are researching it. Document your experiences and just start sharing the academic part of it.

I feel this is the beginning to that path. Hopefully Egypt will reveal so much more than I have uncovered thus far.

APPENDIX

I have spoken with my Jupiter family a lot since our time together. We are all on parallel tracks of ascension with different paths to get us there. We are all equal but each of us has something to contribute to the group. There were a few things that came up in discussions with those folks that I would like to share. Thus, this Appendix is just a collection of things that I have picked up along the way that the reader may find helpful. But I am no "expert" in any of this, these are just my observations.

As in everything; Take what resonates and leave the rest.

GURUS, SAINTS, SPECIAL PEOPLE

I want to start with this because of the importance of DISCERNMENT and keeping yourself safe.

WE ARE ALL ONE AND THAT MEANS WE ARE ALL EQUAL

I don't care what anyone says about anything, no one being is higher than another being. We all come from Source, Spirit, God, whatever your preferred term. Thus, we are all the same, we are all One. If you hurt someone, you are only hurting yourself. Thus, Angels, ET's, Gods and Demons are not higher than us. We are all spiritual beings that come from Source and are living the physical life we signed up for before incarnating. The problem Earth Humans have, is we signed up for amnesia and other entities of higher vibrations did not sign up for amnesia. So, while they may seem more advanced or smarter, it is only because we are staring at a cut diamond set in a ring. We can only see the diamond from one plane or from one side, whereas they can see the diamond and spin it in their hand to view all the sides and facets.

So, if some human claims to be a Guru or the reincarnated King Solomon, or the return of Buddha or Jesus Christ, run, run very far away as quickly as possible. At best they are a megalomaniac and at worst they are listening to a Trickster Entity. Tricksters love to impersonate an Angel or deceased loved one and feed you stories of your importance in this life. They feed the idea that if you listen to what they say, you will be great; they will make you great.

Look around at the Earth Humans that resonate with the Wooniverse a little and you will find plenty of people touting their special-ness while trying to say, "It is not my ego, I'm not special, but I am the reincarnation of Noah, so you should listen to me and what Archangel Michael is telling me." Yeah, okay buddy.

I'm seriously not kidding. There is one dude that I thought was cool for more than a decade. Then he got a rough run of it and started just doing a podcast to make a living and the dude came right out and said I've been talking to this angel, and he says I'm the reincarnation of this biblical character so the president should use me in his Cabinet. He went into a lot more detail with names, but I don't want to out this person, so I'll stay vague. But I instantly used my discernment, and was like, 'Oh, that's why those businesses cut ties with this guy.'

In my opinion, if a non-human Entity comes to you and tells you that you are special for some reason, block them. That is the main playbook in Trickster Entity plans. Whether they want to feed on your energy or the chaos they can make you create, it is not in your best interest to listen to them.

DISCERNMENT.

Just like with our fellow humans, does this entity have my best interest at heart? What angle are they playing? What they want me to do right now won't harm me, but will I be harmed down the road? Sometimes it takes a while before they show their true colors. If you use discernment, you can get out of it when they escalate to manipulation. The problem is the people that fall into the Stockholm Syndrome and won't cut off the evil entity. Just read the Bible, it is kind of one big story about Stockholm Syndrome.

I say this, because of my experience with non-human entities. When I have meditated and met non-human entities, most of them have just been neutral and we have a communication exchange. Done. I never encounter them again.

The couple of times that I have interacted with higher vibration entities that blasted me with pure love energy was the most profound experiences I have ever had. I could not help but break down in physical tears of happiness. I mean tears and snot, crying harder than I did when my two kids were born. In those communications, each time, those entities really impressed upon me the fact that we were equal, and they were not "higher" or more advanced than me.

The one time I did connect with an entity that I believe was a Trickster, started out normal but as soon as it tried to puff up my ego, I stopped and blasted it with all the Heart Chakra love energy I could, and it reeled back in disgust, and I broke the connection immediately.

As you have read in this book, when in doubt, I push my Heart Chakra energy, love and appreciation at the other entity to see how they react. I have also heard that you can imagine pouring frankincense and myrrh over the head of the entity or dumping salt on them and that works in a similar way to ferret out nefarious entities of lower vibration.

I'll just end this rant with; Question Everything.

PSYCHIC ABILITIES

The more I research this, the more that I believe that as children, many of us blocked our ability to sense more of the universe.

Whether it was the ability to see (*Clairvoyance*), because it scared us or adults told us what we were seeing wasn't there. Well, to be fair, it was in our mind's eye so as far as most people were concerned 'it' wasn't there. But some people seem to have a heightened clairvoyance and can see with their visual eyes and not just their mind's eye. Regardless, if an adult, especially a parent, tells our child self-enough times that what we see isn't there, then we are going to believe that, and it shuts down our *clairvoyance*.

Or maybe it was the ability to hear what wasn't there? This is *Clairaudience*. The ability to hear things psychically instead of through our physical ears. Some people will hear it as a voice in their head. I believe the stigma that society puts on hearing voices, causes us as children to shut this down quickly. Today, if you tell a doctor, you are hearing voices, they are going to prescribe you medication. Twenty or thirty years ago, if you told your doctor that, you could end up in an insane asylum or even worse lobotomized.

Maybe as a kid you had the ability to just know things? That is *Claircognizance*; when you have knowledge of something that you don't know, or information just pops in your head. This is an interesting ability because it is so subtle that adults likely didn't beat it out of you. Instead, if you didn't have anyone to explain it to you and that you should trust it, you likely pushed it aside and spent your whole life doing that. This ability, in my opinion, is more like intuition on steroids. But life is difficult, and we question ourselves so easily, that many people with this ability have stifled it their whole lives instead of using it as an inherent cheat code.

The next two Clair's that many more people have than realize compared to those listed above is easily *Clairempathy* and *Clairsentience*. These are related to feelings. *Clairempathy* is feeling information about a place, feeling physical or emotional pain of the land where something powerful happened. Places where the *Clairempath* can feel fear, jealousy, hate, or physical pain that happened in a location. For me it seems to manifest as feelings of dread or nausea when I visit some historical locations.

Clairsentience is a tough one on those with this ability as I speak from experience. This Clair means the person physically experiences the thoughts or emotions of those around them. It means we can pick up on the energy of the people around us. For example, if I walk into the DMV, I'm instantly blasted with feelings of anger, frustration, and impatience. I haven't even gotten in line yet, so I know those aren't my feelings. My son is even more sensitive than I am, so he usually gets overblown before I do when we are in crowded areas.

There are two more clair's that I believe are quite rare. *Clairgustance* is the ability to taste things when you are not eating. So, tasting in relation to an experience, or in a meditation. Then there is *Clairsalience*, or the ability to smell odors that are not present. This might not be as rare as *Clairgustance* since many 'ghost hunters' on TV will report smelling odors that are not present like a cigar or the fragrance of flowers.

After all that I have seen, read, watched, learned over the last forty years of being fascinated by the weird, I believe we all have all these Clair's. But I believe that different Clair's are easier for some and more difficult for others. Where one person might be good at *Clairvoyance* and *Clairempathy*, another person might be good at *Clairaudience* and

Clairsalience. So, I think it is a good idea for people trying to reawaken or unlock their Clair's, to feel into this list and see which one's they think they have. Then focus on developing those one or two Clair's to become stronger. There are an untold number of Light Worker websites out there that offer courses in strengthening different abilities. So, feel out what you think you already have access to and seek out a teacher that can help you strengthen those abilities. Or not.

Now, if you have *Clairempathy* and need help dealing with it, this is what I have found helpful. First, remember the universe is what we make it to be. So, if we believe we can shield ourselves from the energy of others, then we can. Here are a couple of methods you can try to block out the energy of others or just as importantly to block others from drawing your energy. Many of us refer to those people as Energy Vampires. These are important exercises to use before you get out of your car or even before you leave your home in the morning.

A: Envision yourself placing a bright golden bubble around your body to shield the emotions of others.

B: Ask Archangel Michael to place a shape shifting energy shield around you and to keep your energy in the shield and block the energy of others from entering your shield.

C: Just like Iron Man putting on his metal armor, envision yourself putting on an energy belt that goes down from your waist to envelope your legs and feet and from your belt up over your body and out your arms and wrapping around your hands and head. Completely encased in your energy shield armor.

PROTECTING YOUR HOME

As you begin to open yourself up through meditation and thinking about the world and universe in new and exciting ways, other entities will take notice. A good description I once heard was the idea of people as candles. Imagine at night, every living person is a candle, and you can see them through the walls and buildings. No one stands out, they all look like a candle flame. Now, imagine a few people in the sea of candles have a flame the size of torches. These are Light Workers, and they stand out. Really well-developed Light Workers can even appear as bonfires.

Elementals, spirits, ghosts, fae folk, Jin, demons, Extraterrestrials, Inner Earth beings, Extradimensionals, Angels, gods, you name it. If they can see us as torches among the candles, then we need and want to put up shields to hide behind. We want to protect our house, family, especially our children, and our sleep. Here are a couple of methods that I like to use.

A: Acquire five or more quartz crystals, they don't have to be very big or clear, just bulk crystals are fine. Go to the first corner of your property with the crystals and a shovel. Dig a shallow hole. Then, hold one crystal in your hand and say, "Crystal, I ask that you work in concert with your brother and sister crystals to help shield and protect my home. Protect my family and our sleep from any entity that is not of Love and Light." Kiss the crystal and then bury it. Go to each corner of your property and repeat this. Then go to the center of your property and bury the fifth crystal in the center of the lot (*or close to it*).

Once completed, close your eyes and concentrate. Then envision your crystals at the corners connecting to each other. Then the center crystal going straight up and the other crystals going up at angles to connect to the center. This creates a pyramidal shape of crystal light shielding your property. Repeat that envisioning on a regular basis. Personally, I do it every night.

B: I have done a fair bit of work connecting to my Spirit Team. Remember, they are there to help but they cannot help you unless you ask for help because of our free will. You can ask in your mind, but remember, "In the beginning was the word". Words are power, so I believe asking for help out loud is the best. I ask my Spirit Team to help protect our home every night before I go to bed.

I close my eyes and concentrate until I can see my house in my mind's eye. Then I suck in a deep breath and envision a purple egg with dark purple spots. I envision the egg growing out of my heart chakra. I grow it in size until it encases my house with its protection. Then I go even farther by placing my guardian angels around the center of the egg facing outwards. Next, I ask my dragon to post up on top of our barn in the back. I ask my cyclops guide to patrol the front of the house.

Between the crystal grid and purple egg with my guardians, I spiritually feel very safe at night. And since I began this, my daughter seems to have fewer nightmares than she did.

C: Another method that I like is to place a piece of selenium crystal in each corner of my home to help with a barrier around the outside of the house. You can also go all the way and gather enough smoky quartz crystal shards to surround your house on the outside. This is supposed to be a powerful method to block out malevolent spirits.

D: Lastly, I have a large brass singing bowl. I will routinely go to each room of the house and gong the bowl and let it resonate to silence before leaving that room. This is a good way to clear any bad energy you or your children might have brought home. This is especially useful if you have a home office you work out of and if your kids are teenagers. Or if you had someone over with energy you don't find very likable.

E: Every time I bring a new crystal, used object, or antique into my home, I clear its energy. Before bringing it inside, I use a brass singing bowl and its sound frequency to clear the item of any attachments or negative energy.

CHAKRA BALANCING

The energy in our body is a powerful or detrimental thing. If we routinely power up our chakra's and keep our energy flowing, it can help us stay healthy and more in touch with our Clair's and generally happier in life. If we let our chakra's break down, the energy can get stagnant and cause us physical dis-ease.

I balance my Chakra when I get in the shower and when I start a meditation. I even do it when I'm driving or sitting in a waiting room for an appointment.

Here is the method that I follow but there is no right or wrong method or number of Chakras to balance. Please keep in mind that our Chakras have a front and a back. Most people, me included, focus on the front of their Chakras and get them spinning but forget to do the same to the back of their Chakras. A good method for the back of our Chakras is to envision yourself standing in spirit behind your back and looking at the back side of your body and Chakras.

In your mind's eye, envision red roots leaving your bottom red Root Chakra from your tailbone, going down both your legs to your feet. Envision those red roots leaving your feet and going down into the Earth. Send them down, down, down and once they are secure in the ground, picture them curling into eagle talons and anchoring securely to the ground.

Now, return to your red Root Chakra. Envision your spirit holding a stick like a crankshaft on the front of your Chakra and spin it clockwise faster and faster. Then allow your spirit to walk around your physical body and do the same to the back of your Root Chakra spinning it clockwise.

Using that method, next move to your lower abdomen where your orange-colored Sacral Chakra sits. Repeat the process to activate this Chakra. Next move to your sternum where the yellow-colored Solar Plexus Chakra and repeat the process.

Next is the green-colored Heart Chakra. You can activate this the same as the previous or you can try my method. I use this method out in public when I'm in a location with disgruntled people living a difficult life. Of course, before I do this in public, I've put up my invisible energy shield and connect to Source through my Crown Chakra before doing this.

Regardless, during my Chakra balancing, I envision my green Heart Chakra spinning and growing in size. Once it reaches the size of a basketball, I squeeze down this Chakra. As I do, it spins faster and faster and grows denser until it is around the size of a baseball. At this point, I send out my thanks and appreciation to the Universe and the people and entities around me and then explode out my Heart Chakra as an ever-expanding ball of energy that grows outwards like an exploding star.

After the explosion of love and appreciation, I return my Heart Chakra to its normal size and spin speed. Then I move on to my blue-colored Throat Chakra. With my Throat Chakra, I return to my standard method of spinning the front and back of the Chakra in clockwise direction.

I differ from this methodology with my dark-purple colored Third Eye Chakra. Starting in the front of my Chakra, I spin it clockwise and then go to the back of the Chakra and repeat. Then I extend my Third Eye Chakra out in the front and back to a conical shape out beyond my skull. Next, I envision this shape like an old pirate style telescope, and I see the front of this Chakra opening like an eye. Then I open the eye of the back facing telescope. Then, as one piece, I rotate the front telescope to the left

180 degrees. So, the front is now facing back, and the back is now facing forward. Lastly, I spin this form one more time 180 degrees until the front faces front and the back faces back. I believe this allows my Third Eye to see the world in a complete way but also to see things from a different angle to better understand the world.

Lastly, my pinkish, purple-colored Crown Chakra is also unique in its activation. Initially, I spin the front and back of the Chakra like all the previous. Then as it spins, I envision it forming into a funnel-shape that tilts up from the front of my body a complete 90 degrees, so the funnel is facing up. Just like an oil funnel if we were adding oil to my car engine. This allows me to connect to Source from above and give it a path to flow down into my Crown Chakra and into my body down through all my Chakras.

Interestingly, this method eventually caused my Hand Chakras to activate to the point that I can feel the energy in my hands at any time I'm still for a little bit of time. Usually, this happens when I am driving or watching television in the evening. Or it can activate when I'm meditating or around certain crystals.

If I am meditating, this is the first process and then I move to breath work. If I'm showering or just activating my Chakra without the plan to meditate, then this is the full process, and I move on.

MIND'S EYE

Seeing in your mind's eye is a powerful skill to develop. People ask me how to do it, but there are a couple of angles to this. One; keep in mind it is not like watching television, there isn't that level of detail. Two; I think I spent decades unwittingly training for this.

I had a terrible time falling asleep during my teens and twenties and then in my thirties falling asleep suddenly became easy.

Instead of lying in bed for two hours thinking about the day and wishing I could do some of my day over or differently, I dove into fantasy. I would lie down and imagine myself doing something that I really liked. In my youth, I would imagine myself snowboarding. I would picture myself going down the slope, sliding from side to side, hitting a jump, cranking up my speed, getting on a ski lift. I would imagine myself riding the ski lift and looking down at the trails and the different parts that I wanted to ride over. Then before I knew it, I would fall asleep.

In my early twenties I moved to the beach. My pre-sleep fantasy changed to surfing the perfect wave. Sunsets on the beach, dropping in on big waves. Watching bottlenose dolphins swim by me. Seals barking at me to get my attention. My friend's surfing and having a good time.

After maybe a decade of those types of fantasy worlds, I began to picture myself living in true fantasy worlds. Worlds of sword and sorcery, good and evil, knights and princesses. All with the goal of quieting my 'monkey mind' so I could fall asleep.

So, when I began meditating in my mid-forties, viewing things in my mind's eye through consciousness projection, was sort of easy. It just happened without me trying to force it.

If you have a difficult time seeing things in your mind's eye when you meditate or for past life regressions, then I recommend trying this pre-sleep routine. Imagine yourself doing something you love. An activity or an event with friends or family. It is like training your mind to decouple from our 3D world and peek into the astral.

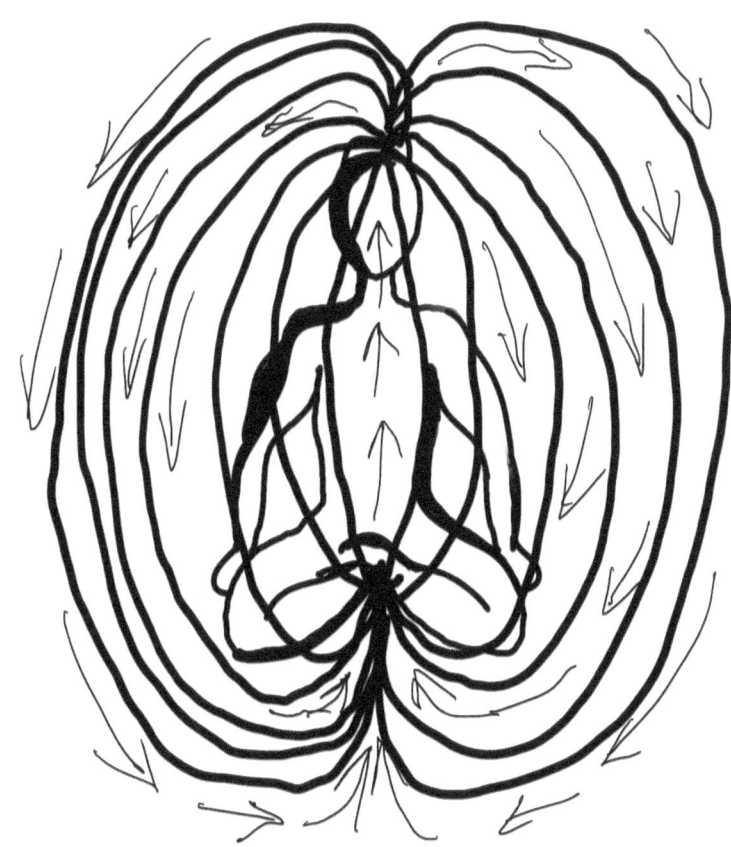

SUPERCHARGE YOUR MEDITATION

There is one thing that I have found that makes it much easier to get to the Delta state of mind and help project my consciousness. This is from Dr. Joe Dispenza's lectures. I jumped on this idea early on because of my penchant for science. He believes that part of getting to this altered state of mind is activating the pineal gland.

The pineal gland, as I understand it, has spinal fluid around it and it connects down the spine all the way to the bottom of our spine in our tail bone. Thus, with a breathing technique, we can squeeze the container holding the spinal fluid and push it up to press against our pineal gland and help activate Theta state and jumpstart our consciousness.

When I meditate, I always go through my Chakras. Once that is complete, I begin a breathing exercise to emulate Dispenza's theory. I take a deep breath through my nose and hold it, tightening my stomach. While I hold my breath, I envision a toroidal field around my body. I picture the energy field starting at my feet, going up my spine to my head, out my crown and along the outer toroid and back down to my feet and into my body again. Think of yourself sitting inside an energy donut. It is a constant swirling up, out my head, down, back into my feet and up again. Then I slowly release my breath through my nose and repeat.

I don't know how many minutes this takes, but when I start to see flashes of orange light behind my eyelids, I know I have reached this state, and I can return my breathing to normal and wait to see what happens.

Enjoyed the Book?

Support the Author by leaving a review at Amazon and Goodreads.

Follow at
YouTube: @dragonclanmedia
Instagram: @dragonclanmedia
TikTok: @dragonclanmedia
Twitter: @dragonclanmedia

ABOUT THE AUTHOR

Matthew was born in California where he grew up fishing and hiking the Sierra Nevada mountains with his father and brother. That would later transition to snowboarding, which took him to live in Switzerland for a winter in college. That was an eye-opening experience for a 19-year-old and made him more open to other people and their views on life. Once he returned to school he focused on the biological sciences where he met his wife of 26 years in chemistry class. From there, they moved to Oregon and Matthew's job as a field biologist sent him all over the United States to conduct surveys on endangered plants and animals. Now settled on the East Coast, he enjoys travel hockey with his two kids and exploring the weird and supernatural aspects of planet Earth and consciousness.

www.ingramcontent.com/pod-product-compliance
Lightning Source LLC
Chambersburg PA
CBHW030909120626
46554CB00001B/73